Lesbian Erotica

Themes With Steamy Overtones Like
First Time and Billionaire

Edmundo Fitzgerald

What could possibly be worse? Me not knowing what you're thinking or feeling, or you not knowing who I am or how I appear. I seem to be speaking to myself. Yes, I do write to you, and because I still see changes in you, I suppose you are still reading. You seem to be developing and gaining confidence. But I don't get to hear anything concrete and honest from you. I can see the physical aspect of you, but I'm unable to interact with it. Despite how much my body desires you, I am not giving in, even though I can. On the other side, you are learning about me without allowing appearances influence your opinion. You may compare it to online conversation without the need to see a profile. However, chatting allows for two-way communication and, from what I've heard, may sometimes result in online sex.

At first, I considered this a clever idea—a special way for me to introduce myself to you. Now, I'm not so certain about it. I hope you don't think of me as some sort of lunatic who is manipulating you in this way.

I've had a long week, and I've only seen you once. It's likely that our timing was inaccurate. At times like this, I wish I could talk to someone about how I'm feeling, have them listen to my complaints and let me vent, and give them a hug and kiss to take away all the horrible things that have happened. Miracles may take place when unconditional love is present. The ultimate objective is that. I want to devote my whole being to one person, shower them with my undying love, and reciprocate in kind. Oh, and there must also be fantastic, earth-shattering, passionate sex, ha ha.

Just having it off my chest has made me feel better. I won't go into specifics, but at least towards the end of the week, things were beginning to improve. I'll be in a better attitude the next time you hear from me, I swear.

Verse Seven

I apologize for last week's rambling style. I spent the whole week feeling down, but suddenly everything is so much better. This week's highlight was spending more time with you. I believe I saw you more this week than I did the two weeks before put together. That has the drawback of making it harder for me to forget about you. When you dominate my thoughts, it is difficult for me to focus on anything or maintain my attention.

I have to keep myself occupied and engaged because whenever I get a moment to myself, my mind wanders and starts thinking about you. To be quite honest, I start daydreaming about you. You are at fault. With the attire you are wearing right now, you continue to tease me. You used to be appealing to me, but now you have my whole attention. Sometimes you dress in a way that is more suggestive of a date where you are attempting to make it abundantly obvious how you want the evening to conclude. Sometimes it's more understated, with your sensuality just barely visible but yet detectable. It's subtle enough to entice anybody without their awareness until they feel their heart beat faster and sneak a stray glimpse. Although it was always there, you needed a person to turn it on for you. You don't need me or anybody else to bring out the seductive confidence you already possess, let me let you in on a little secret. Never again push it away. Let it glisten and glow. Make some people look, but expect respect. Never give up on your heart. Until you are prepared to share it with the person you love, guard and defend it.

Okay, I've had my say for the day. I was lost. Oh, sure, I was referring to the fact that I can't stop daydreaming about you, particularly in that bright white button-up shirt and tight trousers you were wearing. You left the top few buttons undone so that you could see your flawless skin and the top of your gorgeous bra without any obstruction. Your shirt's sharp collar stood in sharp contrast to your jaw's soft curvature. I moistened my lips and let my eyes trace the seam's lower edge as it passed effortlessly over the top of your bra. The cloth itself nearly seemed to be pleading for someone to loosen it where the first button was secured, lying on the cleft between your breasts. I was more than ready to free the small button from its impossible burden before moving on to the next button and so on. As you pushed more buttons, more of you became visible, and I could almost feel the heat escaping from your skin. I would bite my bottom lip to restrain the overwhelming need inside of me to continue until the last button no longer concealed your radiant light. I would move my eyes slowly and steadily up your stomach, the bottom of your bra, slowing down even more to observe the sharp rise and fall of your breasts moving with your quick breaths out of your control, up the flawless skin of your chest, your neck, and chin, pausing briefly on the lips I'm going to kiss and taste, the tip of your nose, before moving on to your intense eyes staring back at me telling me what you are thinking without you having to say a word. Just by gazing into your eyes, I am able to sense your feelings. I nearly can't bear how intense it is. Your face serves as a road map to your bodily wants, and I can read all you are experiencing there. Your slow, forceful swallows, the small tightening of your jaw, and the way your tongue slides over your lips to wet them all show how eager you are for our first kiss. Although you're anxious, you're making an effort to mask it. You've been waiting for this moment for a very long time, so it's not out of dread.

Chap. 3

Say it with me right now, loud and proud, "I'm Never Drinking Again!" You know the old adage that we all use after we've partied a bit too hard the night before.

As she perched on the edge of her little bed, Alison stroked her temples. They reached the date after around three beers. The thrill that had given them their second wind the previous night returned for the date, and Alison flushed to herself. She carefully got out of bed and rinsed the covering of the previous night from her body. Although a little unpleasant, the hot water was really appreciated.

She let the warm water to gently wash her body. She leaned forward with her hands on the tiled wall, each drip following its own path down her curved back. The transparent liquid found its way down her body and made her hair heavy by softly pulling on it. She appreciated the sensation of having a liquid that seems to be empty wash her skin clean.

When she was on her back, she leaned against the wall. The same cleansing hot liquid dripped from her abdomen and onto the ground below after crawling down her shoulders and over her breasts. She stretched, gave herself a thorough scrub from head to toe, and then started preparing her hands for surgery. She has consistently done something out of habit.

She jumped when she heard a knock at the door and yelled! Who the heck else was in the flat where she resided?

Alison phoned apologetic and said, "Hello.

In order to be heard, Kim slightly cracked open the door. I'm sorry to frighten you this morning. Earlier, I called but you didn't pick up. Why was she in this place?

The question "What's up?"

Where is your coffee, I could only find the machine.

What in the world? Alison didn't spend the previous night with her, did she? She had never engaged in a one-night encounter before and always waited until she had an STD conversation with a potential partner before acting.

She said in a shaky voice, "They're in the cupboard over the fridge.

Kim said, "Okay, thanks," and shut the door.

After attempting to remember the night for a few minutes while drying off, Alison left the restroom. She saw Kim seated at the table holding two cups, each of which was steaming and had milk and sugar on it. Kim grinned and said, "Good morning." "Morning," she said with a nod before turning and walking into her room to get ready.

She soon showed there wearing a grey skirt and a purple button-up top. She entered her dining room, where Kim was sitting at the table with a broad grin on her face. "Did you get enough rest?" As she added milk to her coffee, Alison questioned.

"I did, thanks," she answered, turning to face the sofa, where a blanket and pillow were neatly folded and positioned on the middle cushion. "Remarkably comfortable!"

The anxiety she had about the situation vanished for Alison. Everything began coming together by itself. After a couple more drinks and a bite, they departed from the bar. Kim and Alison headed to Alison's apartment after Alison tried to get a taxi for her but ran out of money.

Kim then collapsed onto the sofa. Then, a grin of relief appeared on her face.

It was mildly stimulating to see Kim in the morning, despite the disruption to her daily routine. They made some waffles, spoke for a while, and drank their coffee before rushing out the door. They were driven to work by Alison, and everything seemed fine.

Even though it wasn't uncommon for the hospital, work that day was very frenetic. It was a very typical day with nothing particularly noteworthy. Staci became rather upset at one point because one of the new nurses wasn't properly completing the paperwork. Jenn and Mike joined Alison at the table for lunch, along with another medical professional. Kim wasn't going to join them today since she had stuff to do.

Jenn and Mike were having fun with their new fondue machine. The other doctor started enquiring about Alison's area of expertise and if he might do a fellowship under her. Then, without warning, their phones and pagers started to ring and they were all back at work. Only once did Kim and Alison manage to grab a break together during the course of the next several days. Although it was great, Alison was missing her pal.

It couldn't have arrived fast enough for the date, and boy was it fantastic when it did. The day went very quickly! The transition ended so suddenly that it was almost surprising. That day, she made a brisk trip home, and around halfway there, her phone began to vibrate with the message: U pumped 4 tonight!

Hello from Chez Robérte!

After taking off her clothing, Alison entered the shower. To show off the girls, she donned an off-the-shoulder

Ponte dress with a little split down the front. Black never failed to flatter her appearance, and it also fit her figure well. Sharp, black cat eyeliner was applied while she applied her makeup. Next, a little of red eyeshadow, and lastly, the complementary lipstick. Final verification in the mirror next to the door. To inflate the females' egos or not? Eh couldn't possibly harm.

Kim was at the table waiting when she got there. She got up from her chair and smiled cheerfully as she greeted her date. She was wearing a flowing red dress with blue birds on it and had dark red lips. The tapering top of the dress really enhanced her delicate shoulders. Kim gave her a red wine and added, "You look wonderful.

"I'm grateful. So do you, that's a wonderful outfit on you!" Kim responded to Alison's little embrace by giving her a quick kiss on the cheek. They took seats and took their menus to place their orders. Alison was a bit excited but also quite frightened when she realized it was a date. From her menu, Kim kept gazing up at her and making flirtatious eye contact with Alison. A few minutes later, they placed their dinner order.

Even so, their date was a touch uncomfortable. There was little to discuss since they collaborated on projects. Being friends, they also had a lot of information about one another. They eventually got around to discussing their goals for the future. Alison was determined to pursue her area of expertise and, who knows, one day may perhaps run a department in a major metropolis.

Kim felt it was fantastic that she hoped to one day lead a whole department. The portions of Alison's work that Kim couldn't see were discussed. The processes and the particular pressures in the industry. Kim said, "So, you're a real pussy pro," flashing a sinister grin. "I'll bet you know how to work them better than a cock."

Her small cat may have begun to move at the same time as the worry monster chose to bite her in the stomach. Being on a date with Kim seemed like nothing more than a pleasant evening with her closest friend. However, she was not exactly this. However, she was presently seated across from a stunning, flirtatious lady. She held Alison's interest, which was fascinating.

Her eyes were caught in a playful little tussle with her ocean blue eyes. Before breaking off and beginning again, they continued to gaze at each other with increasing intensity. Alison enquired about Kim's desires in order to release the tension created by that energy. She laughed, wishing she could keep working, be promoted, or perhaps relocate to a better-paying post to become the head nurse. Everything hinged on her ability to continue helping the individuals she desired.

They carried on chitchat about interests and TV series they liked. Kim was perhaps a little bit too into The Big Bang Theory. While completing a couple glasses of wine and taking pleasure in a great supper, small chat resumed. After drinking enough alcohol, the small monster released Alison's stomach. Alison thought Kim was hilarious and that her contagious laugh made her feel happy. She was also attractive, obviously in her element, and very lovely.

After spending about an hour with this lovely lady, something unexpected occurred. After setting her drink down, Alison laid her palm on the desk. Kim extended her hand and stroked it. Alison briefly became silent. The date became abruptly real.

The stunning lady reassured Alison, "Don't worry, it's just a little contact, I've slapped your ass before don't forget," Then, while grinning, she held her hand. Then, her lips parted to let out a long, leisurely breath. How do you feel about yoga, then?

The date went ahead without incident. They conversed, shared beverages, and held hands more closely as a pair. They divided the bill and left a generous gratuity when they departed. Before leaving for home, Alison made the decision to drive Kim back to her house. Holding hands as they both exited the vehicle and made their way to the door was reassuring and helped Alison feel less scared.

Kim turned to face her as they approached the door and said, "So, I had a really good time with you," grinning.

"Me too, it's been too long since I went on a date like that. I appreciate this.

She wanted to kiss Kim, but she didn't know how, and it felt weird. Kim recognized it, was aware of Alison's thoughts, and made the decision to simplify things for her. Kim leaned forward and Alison instantly felt heated. She grabbed the blonde's hands and gently drew her inside. Just before their lips touched, there was a silence, which Alison immediately filled.

Since Alison was used to taking the lead in relationships, she grabbed Kim and their chemistry ignited like the Fourth of July. To begin the second round, they clasped together, their lips locking and then disengaging. In order to prevent Kim from moving, Alison moved her close sparring partner toward the door and slammed her against it.

Their lips were touching, and Kim could feel the lipstick spreading over one another. Two tongues moved back and forth, fighting for dominance. Her cheek was briefly touched by the blonde woman's hand before it firmly gripped her face. Before Alison took a step back and kissed her lips, they had battled back and forth for what seemed like an hour. The ladies were exhilaratedly inhaling, sensing the spark that had lighted the fuse and realizing that they were in for one heck of a performance. But it would have to wait.

The next day, they both had jobs, and the morning would arrive much too early. After one more kiss, Alison received a swat on the behind. She grinned, "Sorry, I'm a bit thrilled. The ladies dispersed in all directions.

It's remarkable how much more open and expressive individuals are when you offer them the protection of anonymity. When Max reviewed the homework from the previous week, she saw that some of the students really do have some type of promise. School must be challenging, particularly in a place like this. Most don't come from the average middle-class British household. Not at all. Both their speech and behavior give you the answer. Some of them must be concerned, but they don't want to participate in class out of fear of what their classmates may think. She was reminded of her own school days and how much peer pressure there is. Max remembered the several occasions when her friends put pressure on her, mainly at parties where they challenged her to kiss males and drink pints of cider. When she realized she was gazing at nothing but a child who should have been in jail, she shivered. Awkward. After grinning at him, she resumed reciting the poem.

It was reasonable to assume that she felt considerably more certain as a teacher after a week. Although she still had some technical things to learn, she mostly succeeded in making connections with all of the courses and some of the students. To avoid becoming one of those obnoxious instructors who used expressions like "Oh you with curly hair," which always felt a little insulting, she worked hard to remember everyone's names. She knew she would arrive before the end of this week, but some came more easily than others.

Some of the material Max has read thus far has been enjoyable. The majority of these poetry dealt with grief and crushes. Some of the topics included mental health problems like sadness and anxiety; it's surprising how much more open people are to such topics now. The name in the upper right corner caught her attention as she picked up another piece of paper. She had the impression of having just finished reading a book. There was a sense of relief, but there was also a hint of disappointment. Max entered the real item to read it.

I apologize for every false statement, dishonest act, and every sentence that entered my head.

I'm sorry you were caught in the force of nature I refer to as my lack of conscience, and I'm also sorry I wasn't able to honor the silent agreement that was formed in the split second between you shouting my name and having an orgasm.

You weren't exceptional, and I'm not even sorry, it's true.

I said, "Frances, mate." Max read this passage many times. Ouch. Identify with the person this is intended towards. Brutal. Knowing who authored this made her feel a little uneasy and like a third wheel.

After putting the poem away, she checked her watch. She stepped outside to the staff room to check if Alan was there since she still had some time before her next session, but it was vacant. Max could hear yelling coming from the girls' restroom. Damn. She was terrified and, to be really honest, simply wanted to go back to class and pretended she hadn't heard anything, but another part of her recalled her chat with Alan about bullies. The door slowly opened, but for some reason it slammed shut.

"Get off me you fucking freak!" she overheard as a wretched cry. Max once again attempted to open the door. She looked up to see a tall, ginger girl looking at her with horror. She saw Francis caressing her right shoulder while lying on the ground with a bloody nose.

"What the heck is going on here?" Max made an effort to seem assured, but she felt very uncomfortable. After a little while, the ginger girl attempted to depart but got no reaction. With her arm, the instructor barred the exit. You must remain here while I seek clarification.

The ginger girl muttered, "Ask this cunt yourself," and shoved passed Max. She was unable to respond in time.

Frances was already cleaning the blood off her face at the sink when Max turned to face her. When the girl attempted to enter the restroom, her body must have banged the door shut.

The instructor questioned, staring at Frances in the mirror, "Did she assault you? "Why?"

Frances disregarded her and began rubbing her blood-stained t-shirt after finishing washing her face. She turned around to go when the stain wouldn't remove itself and flung the paper towel at the mirror, but Max wasn't going to let her. She held the girl's shoulder despite knowing it was not permitted.

Max observed the girl's pupils were much bigger than they should have been when she paused after saying, "Talk to-" Are you impaired?

Frances began this conversation by saying, "Listen," which was the first thing she ever spoke. "You leave me the fuck alone and I won't tell anyone you got physical with me, deal?"

Max gave a headshake. "I believe we have an emergency," She let go of Francis with her hands. "You do realize that you will be dismissed from the school if the administration learns about this?"

Francis scowls.

There seem to be rumors circulating already. How could the girl have failed to see that she was endangering not just her present but also her future? Most likely, the nosebleed wasn't caused by being struck either. Let me assist you.

Frances didn't understand. She didn't feel intimidated or under assault for the first time ever. She questioned if the instructor could be trusted as she met her eyes directly. She neglected to declare her drug usage despite being required to. Why? Frances was aware that the only thing keeping her parents from giving up on her and throwing her out was her attendance at school. She didn't want to be on the street since she had been there two years before, when all of this garbage began. No, she need all the assistance available. She inhaled deeply.

"It's quite reasonable if you don't feel like talking to me. You've never met me. But kindly do not wreck your life. Some of what you are going through, I can relate to. Max was a little uncomfortable to share such intimate details, particularly with a student, but she felt compelled to express her feelings. She was always that moron who felt and spoke excessively. "I'll be marking some work in my classroom after school."

Frances nodded, and Max warily walked away. The young woman turned around and gazed in the mirror at herself. She always looked messy, but this time she felt like there could be a way out.

She started to use the same approach Tina used the week before when I laid down and opened myself to her. I just had to slightly move my head to stare directly at her breasts since she was already starting to get crimson in the face as I glanced at her. She pulled up a wooden stool till she was just in front of me. She sat down and spread her legs and placed her feet up on top of my back while simultaneously reaching back and grabbing the railing. Oh my God, there in front of me, she was spreading her legs. I realized at this point that Tina had told her everything, and everything was public.

I made a minor adjustment and went forward so that I would now fall into her clamshell head first. My fingers and my tongue helped it open by cooperating to achieve a shared objective. I thought she was in a good position. Although it was difficult, she felt comfortable twisting her body like a pretzel. Her breasts were being fully exposed to the sun's rays from above as a result of her arched back.

"I have to admit to you, Tia, that I was unaware that you would be here. It's a nice surprise, and from what I can see, two massage therapists are now interested in giving me a massage. I'm simply relieved that you both are quite knowledgeable, and it helps that you both have beautiful bodies that belong in a model magazine. I stabbed her while listening to the sudden cry she let out as a result of the erratic manner I was licking her.

"Holy sh*t... She seemed to be exaggerating to me, but Kelly, you really do want to be pleased, don't you? Let me tell you, there haven't been many gals in a while who have made me scream like that. Naturally, Tina is an exception to that rule. I didn't need her to say anything else; the way she touched me was just...oh wow...it's like...like...FUCK ME. While simultaneously feeling these needles perform their job, I had every intention of removing her with my fingers. I was still in awe of the needles' therapeutic abilities, and it helped that getting a massage was so soothing it might transport you to another universe.

I have no idea how she managed to maintain her broad, high, and pointed toes for so long, but it was such an amazing feeling that I found myself losing myself in the sensation of her pussy lips being massaged into a frenzy.
You may have differences, but I suppose that is what I appreciate about it. Goddamn it, you are just as delicious as Tina. It provides me with diversity. In addition to using my tongue, I was squeezing two fingers into the wettest, tightest pussy I had ever experienced. Even I didn't have that type of power, and I'm certain that any man who had been given the opportunity to be inside would have wed her then and then. "I suppose you go for guys, then?"

I don't find them very difficult. I'm not saying they don't have a place, however.

God, oh, GodWhere did you pick up this method? When I attempt to woo some of my new customers, I'll have to take it and utilize it. In response to your inquiry, I'm going to fucking CUM. She realized it pretty much right away. "YESSSSSSSS" When I discovered someone else was making noises at the same moment, I recognized it was a bit louder than normal. Both Tina and Andrea had extended their hands beyond a simple leg massage. I questioned if she was simply relaxing since I could hear her faint groaning resonating in the air.

Her mouth was wide, her eyes were closed, and her abdominal muscles were trembling. She let go, and as her fluids poured out into my mouth, I had to keep up with the flow. Even though the stool was trembling from the intensity of the climax moment, I held her down. Her bodily fluids literally spilled onto that wooden bench. My lips were smeared with her substance as I retreated from her. She gave me a kiss while lifting my chin.

I don't know whether I can even stand up, as I was saying before I was so rudely stopped. A guy is excellent as a toy, and I like the expression on their faces when they go far into my cramped, dark interior. I believe it gives me more pleasure to watch as they are completely surprised by how tight I am. It almost seems as though I don't even need them. The excitement of making a lady sexy on the spur of the moment appeals to me the most, and I suppose I've always been drawn to the feminine form. Every time I'm around a lady, there's simply something about her body that makes me want to taste it and touch it.

"I suppose I can see that, but it must be difficult for you to always be around female clientele. With them laying on your table coated with oil, how can you possible finish any work?

Speaking about oil, Kelly. She arose, and I soon felt her bare hands tracing the lines of my back and wrapping their fingers around each protruding needle. A groan was emitted as I felt her fingers on me; this time, however, it was my legs that were opening up. As Tina had done to me before at our last meeting, she quickly started caressing me. "I believe the time has come for you to get compensation. I wanted to satisfy you because of what you done for me. She then gave me an asslap, and I about leaped out of my skin.

Yes, "Oh yeah." I had no idea why I didn't shout instead of saying that. I was essentially requesting more.

"Kelly, I had a very good feeling that you would like it. I can quite accurately predict what women's hidden dreams are. That's what makes me so effective at my profession, and to be completely honest, most of the time it doesn't even seem like work—especially when I sense a lady reacting to me. Everyone should, in my opinion, have a line of work that they see as something they get up every morning eager to do. Additionally, they had to grin as a result of it. It is precious to feel good about being compensated to do what one loves. Your back is under a lot of stress since it seems like you don't love what you do. Would you consider enrolling in my massage therapy program and opening your own practice? I had never given it much attention, but it was an intriguing suggestion.

I felt the oil on my asshole when she spread my cheeks with it and saw that her tiny pinkie was starting to penetrate where no man or woman had gone before. I squeezed, but it didn't stop that small finger from encroaching and making its mark. She started putting two from the same hand into my pussy after she put that one inside of me. She then reached around and put her fingers on my lips while I was effectively having sex in two places at once. Instinctively, I opened them and started to hump my ass against the fingers that had made their way into both of them from my holes. I may not have had all three holes punched with a cock, but they were all filled, and the fire was started from below.

"That's all. Take it in, enjoy it, and think about whatever negative you want. Let go of how much pleasure your body can experience. The same thing I'm doing would be like putting your hands on a lady you shouldn't. Can you picture how it would feel to touch them, then taste them, while observing their body language to see whether or not they are amenable to your advances. The goal is to tease someone until they give in. She was pleasing me in all my holes while I tried to stop myself from thinking some pretty horrible things that I shouldn't have but the feeling was becoming too strong.

"Make me cum...," Although I'm sure you want to, I prefer to feel your tongue to your fingers. My voice was hoarse as I begged her, and I was certain that she was merely warming me up with her fingers in preparation for something a little bit more agile.

They were quickly removed, and she widened and raised me instead, causing my ass to be in the air. When she slipped her tongue into my asshole and let my inner muscles to grip her and keep her inside of me, it was simply like nirvana.

So this is what I get when I have another customer on the go. I guess I can't blame you for that, Tia, because you steal the customers I locate from me. Turning back, I saw that Tina was now grinning and that Andrea's head was resting on Tina's shoulder while she was now partially undressed. Since I've already had her and they're both eager to explore their sexuality, I suppose I shouldn't be too upset. I simply wish I had more time to get the toys out. Maybe another time, and I think you two could need a nice, solid fucking right now.

"I believe that is a fantastic idea." I was attempting to say something, but at least Andrea got in front of me with her point of view. It was really a good thing she did since, much though I tried, I couldn't even form coherent phrases after that pleasure.

"Yes, dear God's mother. YESSSSSSSSSS." I lost it, and I started to roll my ass backwards against her tongue, which was stuck so far within my title hole that I didn't think she would be able to get her tongue out unscathed.

When it was finally over, they both removed those needles, and I stood up off the table and stretched. "I doubt that I could feel much better than I do at this moment. I think I'm going to accept your invitation. I don't want to work on it full-time; part-time is more my speed to start. On the weekends and in the evenings, I'll attend your courses, and after I've earned my certification, I'll start working for you on the side. It will give me the chance to decide whether it's right for me, but if this is any indicator, I would be a fool to not ultimately get into it full-time.

"I see that you have been accepted into my massage school, but at least I can find comfort in the knowledge that you will need to return here for your training sessions. You can't really give them to yourself, and even if you could, the pleasure wouldn't be all that great. As you and Andrea have previously observed in a different manner, it is so much nicer when someone else does it.

"Tina and I will meet you with a surprise at the door the next time you drop by that will stretch the bounds of your imagination. You see, we have certain gadgets and role-playing games that are much too wicked. You two should come over and see them for yourself because you don't know what you're missing. As it stands, I really must get moving since I have a customer waiting for me in 10 minutes. If the lighting are in my favor, it will be close, but I should be able to make it. Together, we all exited with them, and while we stood there, a vehicle pulled up with a young, elegant professional lady in her 30s with a briefcase heading for the door.

I grasped Andrea's hand as we were leaving, and she wrapped her fingers around mine. Knowing that we shared a secret, we grinned. We didn't really need to say anything since our grins spoke for ourselves.

Teased By My Therapist

Kelly had always thought that she should maintain her physical fitness, but lately she started experiencing major injuries as a result of playing a lot of squash. She contacts with a local physician, who advises her that the only effective treatment for this kind of pain, which travels from her neck all the way down to her upper legs, is the use of painkillers. Kelly doesn't want to take painkillers, so the doctor offers her his wife's number, an alternative therapist in the business. She is reluctant to enter a setting like that, but the suffering must be addressed. She discovers not just relief but also a pleasure that can only be experienced by a woman who has the knowledge to understand what a woman wants.

In Chapter 4, we mend broken hearts.

Tamara approaches with two broken open coconuts that have spoons inside. "What's wrong guys?" she asks, sporting a broad smile. She gives Giselle a lips-only kiss. The boys smile when the ladies kiss, and she looks adorable in denim overalls. We live in a planned neighborhood, right?" she asks. What makes that barn in the woods so special to me? due of the large heart on it. "Just because we are more aware and compassionate individuals, doesn't mean we don't sometimes need a gentle reminder, right? We are all under stress here because the environment is different, and we are still getting to know one another and learning how to get along, but we are still in a far better position than the people in the cities who wish they had the courage to do this. She gives Giselle a coconut while grinning.

Bo notices her point as he glances at her. He rests his palm on his chin while he mulls over her remarks. Hey, listen, I'm sorry, he says. I still sometimes feel sensitive and envious. I apologize for being so pessimistic. George continues, "You know, I could have been more considerate too and approached you Bo to see if you like one of these girls or what your feelings were," as he runs his fingers through his long hair. Man, I'm sorry. He extends his arms to you in an embrace. The females give them some coconut as the boys embrace. "Wait!" Giselle has a sore throat, so Tamara advises not to drink after her. Giselle responds, "Oh yeah, sorry!" as she draws her coconut back. "You know, what I've discovered is that we can never act perfectly, but we can be humble, apologize, and try to do things differently the next time," adds Tamara. I am new to this free love thing, so I realize I should have offered to assist more. Guys, I'm still learning. But since I'm a decent person, I don't want to hurt anyone's emotions. The more we communicate, I believe, the better.

The four of them get together and seat down. "Well, you girls are a couple, and that's cool," adds Bo. I suppose if I were to be really honest, I'd have to admit that I don't like being in relationships and that I like sharing intimate moments with a variety of individuals. I've been in relationships with other couples, George claims. I don't have a jealous nature, but I do like some kind of commitment for consistency. I suppose my main preference is for company. Tamara explains, "Okay, so it sounds like it would make more sense for us to stay with George?" This is the strangest discussion I've ever had, but I'm pleased we're having it, Giselle chuckles. I really don't want anything unusual to happen, Tamara explains.

Bo exclaims "ho o pono pono." George responds, "Yeah man." "What's that?" inquires Tamara. It's a Hawaiian prayer for peace, Bo says, and it means "I love you, I'm sorry, please forgive me, and thank you." He sits down and places his hands together while he closes his eyes. "Let's think about it. Men, let's maintain our composure. We are too fortunate to allow our emotions to rule us. When someone is unwell, Hawaii's healing priests put this into effect. The other two sit down and cross their legs after Tamara. I'm extremely pleased we chatted, George says. Everything should be in the open, in my opinion. Bo I am confident in your goodness. Giselle adds as she closes her eyes, "I ask that Tamara and I remember to be grateful and not become selfish among these generous kind souls." The knee of Tamara is pressed. "May we speak with kindness and consider how our actions affect others," she adds. They all get up and embrace, after which the girls go fetch their little amount of belongings and deposit them in George's yurt. He provides them with a dresser for their belongings.

It's nice that the girls feel at ease in his home. The recent arrival of two bisexuals thrill George. He doesn't need to have a lot of sex since he is a patient guy. He takes pride in being a decent person and engaging with others. He gets as fired up about meaningful communication as he does about physical contact. Bo is invited, and he prepares food for everyone. They converse far into the night. Giselle is on the ground seated between Tamara's legs as she sits on the futon. They are at ease. "So when did you girls realize you were interested in girls?" asks George. Tamara explains, "in high school." "This is new to me," Giselle remarks. I spent a few months with a Portland-based woman last year.

With a nod, George adds, "More power to you." So you people want to hear my idea? he exclaims as he becomes animated. They nod their heads in agreement and grin at his excitement. He states, "So I often struggle knowing that we are here in the woods, so happy and healthy in this community but unable to share this way of living with many people." Tamara agrees and remarks, "Yeah, that's a shame, huh?" He continues, "I mean, look at Bo, he can grow a huge garden. We have such simple living." What if we established a non-profit and invited children's groups to see how we live, he asks. They could even assist us with our gardening. Bo's ears perk up and he says, "Hey, that's not a bad idea." George adds, "And we could get grants money to live off of too."

Giselle and I both majored in English, so we can write, explains Tamara. George exclaims, "Really?! That's wonderful!" He scratches his chin and says, "Well, I guess I could pay for a satellite internet service up here so we could do it all without having to go into town." Bo, who is really contemplating something, adds, "This could be really good, but it would affect everyone here, so we would have to ask everyone else what they think you know?" That's a really excellent point, brother, George replies. Yes, we should absolutely contact them. While passing joints around, they lie on the ground and gaze up at the dream catchers that hang from the ceiling. George exclaims, "I love you guys." Bo adds, "We love you too, man."

Giselle puts her arm on Tamara's knee and lays her head on her tummy. Their hands clasp together. "Love is love, right Tamara?" Giselle declares. Tamara responds, "That's right." "Oh man, you guys like oils?" exclaims George. The finest collection belongs to me. He stands up and takes out a large package containing many essential oils. They all slather on essential oils until the whole yurt has the aroma of an apothecary. You know, I'm very excited about tomorrow, Tamara adds. I believe I made progress today. I believe that although I was living for myself, I was secretly thinking about how I might assist others. I wasn't thinking about others; I was just interested in my own pleasure. I believe I'm now prepared to put that compassion to use at this point. To be here with you guys is such a pleasure. I guess you just made me weep, George says. Everyone begins to chuckle.

The next morning arrives quietly as the forest's birds begin to trill. Tamara kisses Giselle's hand before getting up to make coffee for everyone. The females are on the bed, and the two men are seated head to toe on the futon. The calm decision they made the previous evening is still present this morning. While the females hula hoop in the big yurt, the boys get up, stretch, and perform headstands. Their spirit is soothed by music. Tamara takes a drink of her coffee before saying, "I'm ready to get to work, Bo." "Me too," responds Giselle. I must strengthen these hands. After grinning, Bo adds, "Okay, I'll get some gloves." He dashes over to the shed after jumping from the front porch. The other individuals are conversing and preparing breakfast by the fire. There isn't a cloud in the sky when they glance up. "We are thinking about hiking to

Sage Lake and doing acid," the girl with the long brown hair adds.

"Woah for real?" says Bo as he halts in his tracks. "You want to come?" she asks. Okay, if you all assist me in the garden, I can finish sooner, he adds. Do you want to camp there? Young lady nods. With bed hair and a grin while clutching their coffee cups, Tamara and Giselle approach. To avoid scratching up their legs while working in the garden, they opt to wear trousers. The butterflies relax on the blossoming bushes, and they feel the warm sun tanning their skin. Bo teaches them about different plants and how to care for them. Their spirits are soothed by the forest's pure air. As they talk about the educational plan George suggested, they sense a fresh sense of hope emerging. I came to a realization, Giselle explains. All I need is something worthwhile and worthwhile to strive for. I cannot only exist for myself. That is a really simple yet deep insight, Tamara. I'm hot, sh*t!" Giselle uses the hose to wash her down. Her white top has now become wet, exposing her svelte breasts. Bo comments, "Nice."

Suddenly, a girl emerges from the next village. She wears a bikini top and denim overalls with her head shaved. She's got a bag on and sunglasses on. "Hey guys," she exclaims. I wanted to see if I could join you after hearing that you were heading to Sage Lake to take acid. I brought tamales and tequila. Her exotic eyes are penetrating right through Bo, and she has a tan skin tone that is milky and gorgeous. He is struggling to talk. "Of course you can come," he replies. Do you have a tent or sleeping bag? She turns to see the females who are holding hands before turning back to Bo and saying, "I was hoping I could share yours, Bo." Oh really, he adds as he stands up straight and flashes a half-smile. She responds with a seductive grin.

Now that they aren't staying with him, the girls are happy that he has a new interest. In an effort to save water, they immediately rinse off after finishing in the steamy garden. They all departed together into the forest to go as far as their imaginations could take them. As they go, a man is humming. George has no shoes on and has a scarf wrapped over his head. They live in harmony as a tribe of hippies who enjoy life and thrive in the jungle.

"So I spoke to the group, and everyone liked the idea," George adds. Wow, Giselle exclaims, "that's really great. I'm thrilled. "Me too," he adds. I like the concept of spreading awareness of our way of life. "It also will stop us from partying too much, which can also cause problems," he adds. Tamara snickers and adds, "True that." In fact, he adds, "I mean, we could even let adults stay here and camp if they want to just come on a retreat off the grid." After expressing her excitement, Tamara remarks, "You know, I think that could be really healing for some people who get depressed in the city." Okay, George says, "let's visit the village when we get back and check what we need for the satellite internet. This change was made possible by you females. I'm grateful.

Danny

If I didn't already know, Katie was a true sex pot at this point. I had been set on fire by the way she had used her tongue to manipulate my flesh. My whole body was buzzing, and my nipples were erect. I drew her close to me and gave her a gentle kiss as we made our way to the shower. Her magnificent breasts, which were just as perky as I had expected, were revealed as I tugged on her bikini top and slithered it away from her at the same time. Her nipples like two juicy, fully-grown cherries. As she backed into the shower, I caressed her breasts and kissed her nipples.

After giving me a peck on the nose and moving away from me, Katie smiled and started using the shower.

I responded, "I think it's about time you lost these," as the hot water started to shower her.

I held onto the top of Katie's bikini bottoms as she thrust out her rear and performed a small shimmy. It was everything I had not to give her rear a genuine spank since it was so pert and she had such adorable red cheeks. Instead, I squeezed them and then slowly slid one-handedly off my own pants.

I entered the shower where Katie was suggestively pointing the water at her stomach as I emerged from my light blue skimpy underwear. I turned the shower head towards me and slipped my hand up, letting the hot water to wash over my breasts while I pulled the door over. My breasts were covered with a stretch of golden gel when Katie tore off a piece of the soap sachet as she was holding it.

As Katie massaged the soap into my breasts, I put the device back on its hook and pointed it to the side. I covered her tummy with a palm's worth of the lotion and then massaged up between her breasts. We quickly formed a beautiful lather over each other's bodies thanks to the shower's spray, which was just enough to keep us wet without entirely rinsing the soap away. Our lips came together, and Katie responded by pushing her fingers down into my buttocks as I ran my hands over her bottom cheeks.

Our fingers probed as we gave each other a passionate kiss, our breasts squished together in a soapy boob-kiss. Her labia yielded to my fingers like two slick flowers, and her lips were swollen. Katie gasped in the steamy shower as her lips brushed against mine, then my neck, during our frenzied kisses. She crossed our bodies, wanting to get closer to my pussy from the front. I slowly nibbled as her fingers formed a V across my mound while I buried lips on her shoulder. She gently massaged my lips between her fingers while squeezing my vulva, then she traced her index finger up towards my clitoris.

I grabbed her by the hand and drew her in for a kiss. We danced tongues as I turned the shower head in our direction. I grabbed for a sponge as the water splattered over the tiles and started applying soap to her body.

Katie

Danny was incredible. I had no need to worry about approaching her too aggressively after she kissed me and deftly removed my bikini top and bottoms. We began to play and fondle one other in the shower's water, which more than confirmed my suspicion that she wanted me as much as I wanted her.

As Danny massaged the sponge all over and around my nipples, they became rigid and pleasantly tingling. My labia were being caressed while she washed my breasts, and I could feel the tips of her fingers squeezing and pressing at my sex. I yearned to feel her fingers softly slipping in and out and to have her inside of me.

Our tongues continued to dance together as we continued to kiss. My lips widened as I raised my leg up onto her hip and curled it around behind her. Danny gently inserted her middle two fingers inside me as he pushed me again. As they backed in closer and closer, I sighed. Danny slid her index finger across my soapy, moist ring while curling the two fingers already within me against my smooth, velvety inner walls, causing the sigh to change to a gasp. I began to almost reflexively buck against her fingers with my hips in time with her strokes. As I pushed against it, the tip of her index finger slipped barely into my ass. Her other fingers continued to work their way deep inside of me, making little circles over my sensitive place.

My own hands had been softly circling Danny's clit in slow, firm circles the whole time. She seemed to be enjoying what I was doing, as shown by her gasps and moans, but I wanted

Danny to experience the same joy. I slipped my hand behind her and cupped and caressed her ass' pert, slippery cheeks.

My fingers curved across the top of her thigh and around the back. Danny understood what I wanted her to do as soon as I started to gently tug. She mirrored my stance by lifting her leg high and curling it behind me over my hip.

My fingers snaked between her now-spread cheeks and across her soap-stained behind. I carefully inserted my fingers into her while tickling and caressing her ring and slit.

I moved as one with Danny as we shared a passionate kiss. With one leg draped over the other's hip and our wet, soapy boobs pressing firmly against one another, we carefully fingered one other. While hot water from the shower poured down on us, we were submerged in a mist of wet, steaming desire.

Even though Danny and I could have lingered in the shower for eternity, I wanted my tongue to experience all my fingers were doing. I wanted to slowly and sweetly savor every part of Danny's body. I am aware that she shared my desires.

Eventually, between kisses, I gasped, "I think it's about time we went to bed," to Danny.

Bedroom No. 4

Danny

By licking the pina colada off of my skin and by what transpired in the shower, Katie had already given me a taste of the pleasures she had in store. The bedroom was the logical next step, and I was tingling with anticipation. As I entered my room, my pussy hurt and I had tingles all over my body. We continued to steal little kisses in between dabs of the towel as we dried ourselves.

Both the thrill and the air conditioning, which seemed as if it were clinging to my body, made me tremble.

Katie urged us, "Come on, you're dry enough," and with that she yanked my towel from us and encircled us with her own.

Our combined body warmth caused any clamminess to go away as we cuddled. Before moving toward the bed, we stood together, canoodling and stroking against one another. I threw away the improvised robe and collapsed into the bed, using my duvet as a little nest. Katie followed me as we both rolled, and I ended myself on top of her. She had white bedding and her hair seemed like a sea of basalt, and as she looked at me with those brown eyes, I melted. Our lips made contact, and we kissed, sending a million volts through my body. I knelt down and stroked her boobs with my hand while I rubbed my pussy on hers.

Katie made a little noise as I gently kissed her neck. She started to move around under me, squeezing my left leg in between hers. As I gently walked south, I moved my hands over her body, tickling her with my hair as I stopped to place little kisses on her breasts and tummy. I kept going until I was curled up on the bed with Katie, kissing the delicate skin between her thighs. I extended my hands, and as I kissed her pussy with my lips, our fingers clenched together. I divided the lovely petals with my tongue as I rolled it between her sex groove, nudging her clitoris with my nose as I did so. I licked her lightly, bringing the edge of her labia between my lips, and then used the tip of my tongue to go further. With her other hand caressing my hair and her other hand still grasping mine, Katie uttered a wistful groan of delight.

I stood up, and Katie met me halfway. We then alternated between sitting and lying on the bed while we kissed and fondled one another. Katie pulled me back into the bed after giving me a little wink as I attempted to draw her closer to me. She came over on one knee and straddled my shoulders, and as she did so, I immediately realized what she was doing and my pulse raced. She placed her gorgeous cheeky bottom and pussy over my face as I gazed up. I shrieked uncontrollably as Katie licked my secret area even though I could feel the palm of her hand on my pussy. My entire body longed for her tongue. As I dug further, I started to taste her fluids, and a little drip of nectar formed on my tongue.

We soon both started shaking as our climax drew near. My hips were twitching, and I was losing myself in Katie's pussy as my pussy surrendered to her tongue. My body was experiencing its own crescendo of pleasure as my whole concentration was directed upon gratifying her.

Katie

It was pure ecstasy to have Danny's tongue within my pussy. In an effort to get her tongue to caress and probe me further and deeper, I continued pressing my hips up into her face. I was so dripping wet that I couldn't help but spin my hips in tiny circles while stroking my sex all over her face.

Danny was delicious. I gave her a kiss and nipped her clit before opening her lips and sliding the flat of my tongue up and down them. Her sticky, delicious secretions were released for me to enjoy as the tip pushed and wiped at her sex. I kissed and stroked her, inserting my tongue as deeply as I dared. She wriggled and panted under me as my finger tickled and rubbed at her ring the whole time.

Danny and I both felt tense. Even though I was aware of how close we were, I still wanted to give her a passionate kiss when we ultimately reached our climaxes.

After turning around, I kissed her one more while tasting Danny's lips. Before I dropped my pussy to hers and raised her leg onto my shoulder, our tongues momentarily swirled together.

As my pussy touched Danny's, I was overcome with passion. The same way I had done on her face, I circled my hips over her, but this time, the sensation of

Danny's moist lips gliding over mine pushed me to the brink of pleasure.

As we rubbed against one other in a frantic beat, the more I pushed Danny, the harder she pushed back. My breasts swung in front of me in sync with the motions of our hips as Danny grasped and squeezed them. As Danny and I made love to one other, my hands were firmly gripped on his, tugging and massaging her nipples.

I leaned in for one more long, passionate kiss with Danny, after which I sat up straight and placed all of my weight on the now-frantic massages I was giving Danny's pussy. The experience was made much sweeter by the honey that was almost spilling out of me and mixing with Danny's own delicious nectar.

She began to pant as Danny fixed his gaze squarely on my. She was just as eager as I was to give in to the sexiest, wildest orgasms. Before letting go, I gave Danny one final strong shove. I let out a loud gasp as my orgasm began. As she achieved her own climax, Danny's breath became short and harsh.

Through our climaxes, we kept circling and rubbing against each other because we didn't want to let go and wanted to savor the sensation for as long as we could.

After sharing the most intense and passionate of orgasms, we ultimately fell to the floor in a tangle of arms and legs on the bed.

I gave Danny a bear embrace. I didn't want to let her go at that particular time. The whole day had been the most intense and unforeseen of experiences. Danny was just right, and I didn't want our recent exchange to end there.

Danny

As I shared the moment with Katie, I hugged her close to me. I entwined my legs with hers after removing my feet from the tattered duvet. As I moved Katie's hair away from her face, she blinked slowly and sleepily. As we kissed, I grabbed her buttocks while tiptoeing my other hand's fingertips down her back, following the seductive groove of her spine. She gave me a delicate kiss with her soft, giving lips as she experienced the full delight of perfect love.

In the little space between our bodies, she touched my tummy while we exchanged glances, our eyes communicating more than any combination of words could ever hope to. Before giving her lips another gentle kiss, I kissed her forehead and the tip of her nose. She then turned to face me and smiled sweetly. I wanted to remember her face even though I would enjoy the time we had spent together. I would hold in my heart the image of that lovely, heavenly look.

We lay there, Katie twirling my hair in her fingers while I drew fictitious, haphazard designs on her stomach with tiny circles on her flesh.

I finally said, "I could lie here all day."

The next day, Lily discovered herself being silently driven by Emma to an unidentified location.

Again, won't you refrain from telling me our destination? You never offer me any background information regarding any case, even though you don't want me to seem confused in front of the victims.

"I find it to be really dull. I really detest that portion of the job description. However, you are correct; you have a right to know, Emma replied as she rounded a corner.

"So? What's our destination?

"We are seeing a lady named Sally Mathews at her home. She was raped last night during a robbery by a masked guy who also stole all of her stuff. We're heading there to get some answers to some follow-up inquiries as well as for moral support. That's all I'm aware of.

The police patrol vehicle made another right and drove into a neighborhood that was surrounded by tall oak trees and had groomed gardens in front of contemporary white homes.

Lily questioned, "The woman lives alone?"

She is divorced, and her 19-year-old son, who is her sole child, has recently started college. As can be anticipated, the lady is very upset and will need emotional assistance. Emma gave Lily a sideways look, "Do you think you will be able to handle that situation if it arises?"

Naturally, I will. Emma, I hope you don't see me as a weakling since I had a panic episode the day before. That incident was isolated. You are aware that I am more than capable of managing these circumstances. I merely...wanted... I only wanted to impress you, and see how that has turned out, Lily continued, her voice shaking and her chest tightening as she struggled to finish her sentence. She then collected her courage, glanced at Emma, who was also staring at her, and added, "I just felt like choking up, but look how that has turned out."

Then you should have not lied to me, Emma remarked in a cold, calculating tone as she removed her eyes from Lily and looked straight ahead at the road.

***

Before Lily and Emma, Mrs. Sally Mathews sat on a chair with three other ladies; two of them were nurses, and the third was a relative, a distant cousin.

The enormous bedroom in which they were currently seated had floor to ceiling windows on one side, soft beige carpeting throughout, and a luxurious circular arrangement.

Lily fixed her gaze on the lady, who had red shoulder-length hair, narrow, wiry lips, and a sharp nose. She seemed to be in her early forties. The woman's mood was melancholy, to put it mildly, and it was clear that she had been weeping a lot lately.

Asking "Mrs. Mathews, how are you feeling right now?" Lily heard the lady's concern and sympathy in her question, and she instantly felt an emotional surge for Emma as she saw the usually severe woman reveal a softer side.

How do you anticipate me to act? Has the bad guy been apprehended by police?

"No, not yet, but be confident that he won't be hidden from us for very long. All city entrances and roads have already been blocked off, and a manhunt is actively taking place there as well.

Sally murmured, staring out the window with her dead eyes, "I want him to try and flee.

Lily questioned, "Why?"

"I want him to make an effort to elude the police so they can shoot him," I said. I don't want to put him to the test. I am aware of how much time a trial will take to provide justice. Sally added, "I want him dead as quickly as possible. Her cousin was seated on the chair next her and retained her hand and gave it a gentle squeeze.

"I recognize your sentiments, but I respect the law of the nation. I'm Mrs. Mathew. Would you mind answering a few questions regarding the event, please? If you'd like, we can arrive later.

Will it aid in the capture of that jerk?

"Yes."

So go ahead and ask, officer.

***

Do you feel okay? As the two of them left the Mathews home, Lily questioned Emma.

Both yes and no. How is this even possible? How is it possible to be so cruel? How can you include that, and the way the lady simply sat there, stone cold, detailing in gruesome detail what was done to her? Fuck, I can't even think about that. That was one powerful lady right there.

Emma climbed into the driver's seat when Lily unlocked the door to the passenger side of the vehicle. But surely you've seen a lot of situations like this before.

Yes, but I have never heard a victim describe the experience in such a chilly manner. It was unsettling. What about you didn't it affect?

I told you what happened to me was an isolated incident, Lily said as she buckled up and switched on the engine.

In my life, I have seen worse. Anyway, you seem a bit uneasy. What about a beverage? You seem to be in need of one. The day is nearly done, in any case," Lily replied.

"Yes, I'd like a drink."

Can we first get changed at the precinct? Because of our outfits, I don't want people to gawk at us when we enter a pub, remarked Lily.

Yes, and I really loved the outfit you wore when you arrived this morning. You seemed quite attractive," After hearing Emma's praise, Lily's shapely lips curled into a cute grin as Emma stared at her waist, her boobs snugly tucked in her uniform, and her waist.

***

With their police uniforms removed and donning attire that didn't really stick out, Lily and Emma entered a cozy small tavern a short distance from their station.

But because of how they both appeared, Emma and Lily agreed that the other lady stood out.

Emma was utterly enthralled by her youthful companion and how she could go from a capable, shrewd police officer to a thing of stunning beauty.

Emma followed Lily inside the pub while her eyes lingered on the girl's legs, which were nearly fully exposed due to the little pleated miniskirt she was sporting.

She had never seen legs that were so flawless, as if an artist had created them for a comic book in which Lily portrayed a superhero.

She seemed to be an angel from a fairy tale since even her hair, which was often pulled back into a ponytail, was free of their foundations and flowed flawlessly straight beyond her angular face and past her ideal jawline.

If you considered tight leather trousers, heels, and a strapless crop top to be "regular clothes," Lily had never before seen Emma in such attire.

Emma seemed to be the most powerful woman in the world to Lily that evening because she was aware that underneath the attractiveness of her physique and the kindness of her brown eyes was a very cruel policewoman who, given the opportunity, could take on any man or woman and leave them pleading for mercy.

"Beers?" As they sat in a cozy area with a little lamp casting a gentle golden light on their faces, Lily questioned them.

"Whiskey. Beers have no effect on me.

After returning with two Jack Daniel's glasses and placing them on the table in front of Emma, Lily nodded.

I mistook you for a whiskey enthusiast, Lily remarked.

However, I didn't misjudge you.

I don't often drink whiskey, but fuck it, I've gone through a lot myself lately. Could as well.

"You have never swore in front of me before. It sounds strange coming from your mouth," Emma said.

"Why?"

"Because your face exudes a lot of innocence. And a really relaxed attitude.

And also because you haven't cursed once since we first met, which is another reason.

"If I get any more whiskey in me, I might do even crazier things."

"Like what?" you ask. Emma furrowed her brow.

It's "something wild."

Give me an example. Before I attempt to make you drunk, I want to know what to anticipate.

"Umm... I may try to woo you. Maybe express my admiration for your personality to you.

You haven't really spent much time with me, girl, have you? "My personality?" said Emma with a smile. How can you know my personality so well? Perhaps I only have one, and I simply conceal it extremely well.

"No, I don't need more than two days. You come off as someone who is really combat-tested. But I could see that you were worried about the lady we met today. When Lily stated this, Frank Sinatra began to play on the bar's jukebox. "I saw your soft side in action, and I love people who can be hard when the situation demands it, but always have a little corner in their heart where they also have compassion," she remarked.

You've been researching me, then?

"More than you know," Lily concurred.

"Why?"

"Because you're interesting to me."

"Why?"

"Because...you are different from every woman I have ever met," she said.

Lily smiled back at Emma as she peered into her eyes, but Emma was speechless at that point and just took a drink of her whiskey.

Emma questioned, "Why are you playing this game, girl?"

More information about your boyfriend? What led you to him? Eva enquired.

I don't want to discuss him right now. I wish to discuss other topics.

"Okay, then take the initiative."

"I like when someone else takes the initiative. Frank Sinatra's voice swelled in the background, melting like honey in Emma's ears, "I truly enjoy it when I have no control over anything.

Funny thing is, I like having control. Emma said in a sultry voice, "I enjoy it when I can convince someone to do everything I want.

Lily felt her heartbeat pick up.

"Then take command. Why are you holding out?

I need a signal from you, Emma reasoned.

Emma suddenly became aware of an oddity in their immediate surroundings. There were barely any guys in the pub, and ladies were seated at every table.

A few feet away, two late-thirties ladies stood up and lurched toward the bar. They were obviously inebriated.

With their long skirts and full-sleeved sweaters, they both had a very suburban appearance. However, as they got close to the bar, the taller of the two drew the other lady close and started passionately making out with her.

Emma was shocked when everything suddenly made sense.

They were both at a lesbian bar.

"Lily, why did you bring us here?"

The question "What do you mean?"

"I mean, why are we currently seated in a lesbian bar?"

"Are we? I was unaware," Damn, this is genuinely a lesbian club, Lily thought as she tilted her head and swept her gaze around the establishment. Well done, huh? You may bring a lovely woman home tonight. Maybe she'll give that wonderful ass of yours a few treatments in bed to help you forget the bad day.

Do you want anything to happen between us, Lily? Emma said as she sat back in her chair, crossed her arms, and cocked her head. Did the tiny lapdance make you question your sexual orientation? Would you want to play with my ass?

I'm sorry, Emma, but I have no interest in you. Lily laughed heartily, and it took her a few seconds to stop. Even though you are really sexy, I don't like females that act like way. The lapdance just served to underline it. I didn't experience anything; instead, I had a panic attack. I'm sorry, but that is not the case, Lily remarked, looking over at the two ladies who were now having an even more intense kiss and cuddle, with one of them clutching the other's ass.

"Don't you wish you were one of those women, do you?"

"You're crazy. I simply stare at them because I really like how much they adore one another. My heart is becoming mushy from the inside out.

"And is your pussy wet?"

Lily's grin vanished as she quickly turned to face Emma.

"Emma, one last time. I'm not interested in you or ladies. This is a lesbian bar, something I was unaware of. Please put it down now.

Emma continued to fix her intense gaze on Lily.

"You like it when others take the lead. Therefore, you cannot just inform me that you want a relationship between us. You demand that I push you to do it.

You want me to speak out more. You prefer that, don't you? When those college females tried to force themselves on you, you learned that. You were taken aback by how seductive their dominance made you, but for some reason, you pushed that memory and that sensation to the back of your mind. However, the lap dance brought it back to your attention. and you're craving it now, right?

The only sounds in the pub were people conversing and the groans of the two ladies who were still fighting like two beasts when Frank Sinatra had stopped singing.

"I'm not sure I can handle it any longer. I'm sorry, but despite my best efforts to convince you of the truth, I don't believe you will. Lily quickly rose up and said, "I guess I'll leave now. Before she turned around and marched out, Emma was certain she saw Lily grin a bit.

Something overcame Emma as she saw Lily walk away, and as she saw her hips swing and her tall, athletic form move away from her, she too got up and chased the young girl.

By the time Emma caught up with Lily, she had already left.

Without any prior notice, she grabbed Lily by the wrists, dragged her into a small alleyway next to the pub, and shoved her up against a wall.

You will have this if that is what you desire, bitch. Quit making fun of me like this. Look at what you have accomplished now. You will now be treated like the slut that you are.

Lily said, "Don't do it, Emma," as Emma squeezed her body against her and raised one leg in the air.

"You are also a policewoman. You are not a helpless victim. Fight me, then flee. You are a child. You are capable, I am sure. If you don't like it, leave me. However, if you want it, don't stop what I'm doing, Emma replied as she put her lips to Lily's.

Lily resisted and attempted to shove Emma away from her, but she was aware of the futility of her actions.

Emma bit down on Lily's lower lip, rubbed harder against her body, and then slipped a hand between the folds of her skirt.

Emma's tongue shot inside Lily's lips as she opened it and started dancing madly alongside Lily's.

Emma's hand started petting the leg that was around Lily's waist and quickly made its way to her drenched underwear.

Oh my god, you're so dripping wet. Have you not always desired this? Do you like this public humiliation that you are experiencing? Or would you have wanted to have sat next to me in our police cruiser, where you could daydream about having my fingers enter your crotch?

When Lily heard what Emma had just stated, she groaned. She was now making more of an impression with her words than her kisses on her neck.

"Screw me. Put your finger into my leaky puss. Like the slut I am, fuck me.

"No. I'll act anyway I like. I want your face between my legs right now. I want to choke off your lovely, heavenly face. Put yourself on your knees.

However, the alley is filthy. My knees will also get filthy.

"Do I seem like I care, slut? Get down," Emma said, grabbing Lily's head behind and forcing her to her knees.

Lily grudgingly agreed.

In order to pull her panties down, Emma unzipped her leather trousers.

She then took hold of Lily's head's back once again and pressed it up to her crotch.

Emma turned around and leaned against the wall as Lily felt her lips make contact with Emma's hot pussy. Lily, who was kneeling with her tiny skirt up, could do nothing but start kissing Emma's lips.

"Ah, absolutely. It feels wonderful. I wanted your face on my pussy as soon as I saw it. It's like receiving oral care from Kendall Jenner, fuck! "Lick it more vigorously!"

At that same moment, Lily had an internal rupture that caused all of her horniness and sensual impulses to abruptly vanish. She started to struggle with Emma's pussy, but the kid Emma had on the back of her head was too powerful.

"Lily, what's wrong? You don't like the pussy of your partner?

I'm done, Lily murmured, turning to face Emma. I'm not going to do it.

Emma said, "But I'm not done," and she immediately started grinding her pussy on whatever area of Lily's face that came in touch with her crotch.

Emma fucked Lily's face with unbridled fury for a brief period of time while grinding and moaning as if she were possessed, but Lily was stronger and managed to push against Emma's hand to free herself.

Before Emma could attempt to intervene, Lily had already begun to flee. When Lily had turned the corner and was no longer in sight, Emma simply stood there with her back to the wall, her trousers around her ankles, and tears streaming down her face.

She had violated a control she had exercised for years.

As soon as she set eyes on Lily at the shooting range, she did something she knew she might do.

***

a decade ago.

Arts College Dwenny.

Class Room 1.

The females who had been harassing Lily ever since she entered Dwenny broke through the entrance of Lecture Hall 1 and entered.

In the hopes that the girls would leave her alone if she avoided making eye contact, Lily glanced up from her book before returning to reading Shakespeare.

The girls' giggling could still be heard all around her even though the classroom was empty.

She could hear approaching footsteps. She was seated in the back of the classroom when someone ascended the stairs.

"What are you reading over there?"

Tracy, the blonde head cheerleader, was staring down at her with her large, green eyes when Lily glanced up.

Shakespeare, said Lily.

"Really? Then why?

Because it's in our curriculum, perhaps?

"You'd be aware, wouldn't you? Anyway, I guess the ladies and I just wanted to say that we're sorry for being such jerks the last few days. We had never seen a girl as beautiful as you be interested in anything other than suckling every football player, after all. I suppose we were only delineating our boundaries. Or I was, as you are aware that these chumps follow my commands to the letter.

It's OK. Can I resume reading now?

"Of course you can, yeah. However, I've got a better deal for you. Would you want to drive my Ferrari around the block? We can have ice cream in the mall. I owe you at least that much.

"You're not required to do that. I'd be happy if you just left me alone, Lily replied as she closed her book and got to her feet to get out.

However, Tracy grabbed her hand.

"Please? I feel awful about how I've been treating you. You won't need to be concerned about getting bullied once again since there won't be any other girls with us. Please?"

Tracy caught Lily's attention with her green puppy eyes and the way the sunshine shining through the windows put her amber hair on fire. Lily then realized why she had always had the greatest crush on Tracy, despite the fact that she had caused Lily a lot of trouble over the previous several weeks.

Lily answered, "Okay," almost immediately regretting her words.

When Lily and Tracy climbed into Tracy's Ferrari in the college parking lot, there weren't many other vehicles present.

Where are we heading, then?

Lily's heart softened when Tracy said, "The mall," and grinned.

As the sun started to set behind the hills above the village of Dwenny, the

Ferrari accelerated out of the parking lot.

"Can we just stop by the sorority house for a moment? I just need to change into a nicer outfit. I can't simply wear shorts and a sweatshirt to the mall.

Lily objected, "But you didn't mention that at the beginning."

Lily, "Oh, come on. Be not frightened. It's not a crack house; it's simply a sorority house. You'll be all right. You could even win over a few gals and get a sorority invite.

I say, "I don't want to."

Oh, you'll see when you see the home.

Actually, the home was rather nice. In a gated neighborhood where homes resembled mansions rather than typical fraternity or sorority houses, Lily quickly desired she lived in one of these enormous buildings, even for only a short time.

Tracy motioned for Lily to enter and said, "Come in." A big black wooden table stood in the center of the circular foyer, which had halls branching off in all directions.

While Lily followed Tracy down the hallway to the right, she took in the big paintings, chandeliers, and mirrors that ran the corridor's whole length.

At the very end of the corridor, Tracy finally unlocked a door and stood aside to let Lily through.

Lily then felt the chloroform-laced cloth brush up against her nose.

At that point, everything became dark.

When Lily eventually opened her eyes, she saw that she was bound, on a huge king-size bed without a frame and surrounded by three females, one of whom was Tracy.

When Lily understood what had occurred, she screamed in panic, but the gag in her mouth prevented the sound from leaving her throat.

"The geek who aspires to be the popular student. Unfortunately, there is already one at this school. What was James' opinion of her, Carrie?

"That new female is one gorgeous woman, he added. She has a model-like face and a swimmer's figure. Carrie, a short but lovely female with a long ponytail, remarked while grinning, "He virtually got a hard-on while he was raving about her.

"Yes. Yes, he did really say that, didn't he? Do you, you little slut, know who James is? He is my future spouse and the state's governor's son. You pitiful little bitch, you made him lust for you, Tracy said as she smacked Lily across the face.

Lily's cheeks burned, but there was nothing she could do to stop it.

Tracy ordered her two henchmen to "undress her," and they started working. They tore apart Lily's summer dress, tossed it aside, and left her on the bed, nude and ashamed, with tears streaming from her eyes.

Do you like females? Tracy questioned while stooping over Lily.

Lily attempted to speak, but all that came out was an inaudible mumble.

Lily's gag was yanked out of her mouth by Tracy, who then knelt down even lower to give Lily's face a wet, sloppy lick from chin to forehead.

You are delicious! You are going to appreciate being subjugated by me, nerdy squirrel. Your breasts are very adorable. Have any of these nipples ever been sucked on? Has a female ever sucked on these nipples? I have another query.

"Tracy! As you said, This is not necessary. Lily begged with the chains holding her wrists to the bed's golden grills, "Please let me go."

"I'll take it as a rejection. You see, I'm afraid my partner could have feelings for you. But you don't realize how much I've wanted you. My pussy leaks every time I see you march down the hallway in your big sweatshirt and your owl specs, despite the fact that you may have made my relationship difficult. You seem like a helpless little bird that I want to abuse and degrade to no limit, fuck. And what's this? That is precisely what I'm going to do, Tracy said with a sudden ear-to-ear grin and strident tone.

The question is, "What are you going to do?" In a trembling voice, Lily enquired.

Use you as I see fit. Lily, I want you to work for me today. I want you to revere me in the same way that other females do. Lily pointed her finger towards Carrie and the other girl, who was taller than any of them, with straight blonde hair, sculpted cheekbones, and a square chin. "How these two worship me," Lily murmured.

The tall blonde licked her red lipsticks and asked Tracy, "Should we get her ready for you, Mistress?"

"Yes. That would be a wise decision. Make certain her pussy is completely moist. It makes me so happy to see straight females progressively go in to the notion of having sex with another woman. Sad to say, you will get suffering and disgrace from us today rather than love. Girls, you may now start, and I will just stroll over here and take in the show for a while," remarked Tracy as she made her way to the sofa in the room's corner and crossed her legs there.

"No! Please! NOO!"

"Lily, don't squander your energy. She will get more seductive the more you scream. The little girl with a ponytail, who remarkably resembled Ariana Grande, remarked, "Now, let me just take these off," pulling off her top and sliding out of her skirt.

Then, while Lily was still able to resist, Carrie climbed onto the bed, crept toward Lily on all fours, and lay flat on top of Lily.

"You enjoy how my naked flesh feels on yours? Like how our boobs are pressed together, do you? You wish, Lily, that I run our nipples together? Lily heard Carrie purr in her ears.

Lily stopped squirming at this moment and closed her eyes. She made an effort to disregard everything that was happening to her.

"But let's kiss each other first. You ought to be aware of the pleasure having a girl's lips all to yourself may provide. Lily, take a bite of mine.

Lily enjoyed the sensation of Carrie's lips pressing against hers right away.

She had always missed a guy's softness while giving him a kiss.

Lily's bottom lip was first bit and then sucked on by Carrie, who then attempted to insert her tongue into Lily's mouth.

However, Lily made it challenging by not allowing her tongue any room to go about.

Looking at the tall blonde, Carrie said, "She won't open her lips. You'll have to do something to get this bitch to do it. She apparently doesn't want to eat my tongue. She should realize by now that her wants and will have no impact on this situation. Come on, Kelly, just do what has to be done.

Kelly herself sprang onto the bed and immediately went for Lily's breast, which she seized in her mouth and bit forcefully.

Carrie slid her tongue into Lily's mouth as she screamed.

Tracy smiled, rubbed her pussy, and moaned Lily's name in the corner of the room.

Kelly continued to bite Lily's nipples till her areolas became crimson. Despite Lily's pain-induced moans, Carrie continued to lick and tonegu Lily's mouth.

"Pussy her up. Does it rain? Tracy queried.

Kelly felt the stickiness attach to her hand as she stroked Lily's crotch with her palm.

She is wet, Kelly said, sucking the pussy juice from the palm of her fingers. "Mistress, I think you should come and have a taste yourself," Kelly remarked.

Tracy got up from her chair and made a seductive approach to the females on the bed.

Start spitting on her face, Carrie. then lick it off her face before continuing to spew. Kelly, didn't you always say that you adored this bitch's genitalia? They are all yours, then. Take a big bite and forcefully inhale them. Set them up straight.

And what are you going to do, Mistress?

While making her way toward the other females, Tracy paused close to Lily's legs.

It's moist on this harlot. She has become moist as a result of her enjoyment of our treatment of her. She is drenched because she enjoys being controlled by her Mistress. by a lady. And all I want to do is bury my face in her long legs for the first time ever to make her cum for a female.

And she really did it.

While the other females started doing as Tracy had instructed them to, Tracy attacked Lily's pussy.

While Lily's wrists and legs were restrained, three females started abusing her in the most heinous manner.

Lily was anticipated to feel awful. Lily was meant to be experiencing trauma, so why then did she start immediately wailing with pleasure?

Even though she had just recently met the girls, why had she suddenly begun mumbling each of their names?

Lily could only scream at the top of her lungs, "HARDER, HARDER,

HARDERRR" after a few minutes, when three of Tracy's fingers were lodged within her pussy.

Section Three

Lily awoke abruptly.

She couldn't tell whether the sound of anything or the dream had startled her up. Or did she dream about the noise?

Before the doorbell rang, she laid in bed for a little period of time.

It was 11 o'clock at night when Lily glanced at the clock on her nightstand. She had escaped Emma and the alley a short while before.

Lily went to her apartment's front door and peered through the peephole.

Emma answered.

The question "What do you want?" Without opening the door, Lily questioned.

"Lily, I've come to apologize. I have trouble falling asleep. I feel too bad about what I did.

Lily considered her next move as she stood behind the door, her pulse racing.

What if you give it another go?

I am not a rapist, Lily, for the love of god! And you have more than enough self-defense skills. Just let me apologize and then open the door. You have no clue the struggles I'm now facing.

Lily inhaled deeply before opening the door.

Emma was standing at the doorway, sopping wet.

Emma saw Lily's perplexed expression and remarked, "It is raining."

"Enter then. You must be cold. Give your jacket to me.

When Emma entered, she removed her jacket and gave it to Lily.

Lily slammed the door behind Emma and said, "Fuck, the water has leaked in.

"I have additional bathrobes and towels. I'll put your clothing in the dryer once you take them off. I don't want to be the cause of your illness.

"You're not required to do that. You're too lovely to be this way. Emma remarked, frowning. "It's just making me feel worse," she said.

"Listen, I get it. I can't totally blame you. At first, I was having fun with it as well. Simply put, you ought to have stopped when I stopped finding it enjoyable. Anyway, whatever. Things happen. And I can see that you're unhappy about it. I'll go get you a towel immediately. Also, a robe.

***

Emma joined Lily at the little dining table set up in the open kitchen. "My granny taught me how to make the most perfect Hot Chocolate in the world," Lily remarked.

Emma agreed after taking a drink. "And it actually is," she said.

The last thing she needed at the time was for the robe to fit her wonderfully and smell like Lily.

For a few minutes, the two drank their hot chocolate in silence while the apartment's windows were battered by heavy rain.

Both sometimes tried to sneak a glimpse at the other but would turn aside when the other spotted them.

Emma was unable to stop. Lily was too stunning to ignore, and she could not help but notice Emma's stunning boobs poking out from beneath the robe as she wore a very seductive satin nightdress that fell just below her hips.

Emma questioned, "So, where is your nephew?"

He departed.

"Okay."

again, nothing.

"Lily, I don't want things to be this way between us. I don't want to feel uncomfortable. Let's simply address the issue that is most important.

"Haven't we discussed it already? I said that I am now OK.

I do, however, have some further queries.

"Are you speaking as the policewoman in you?" Do you want to question me? As the sound of the rain hitting on the windows became louder, Lily questioned while crossing her legs and enjoying her hot chocolate.

"No. I'm asking you out of friendship. I really hope we're still close.

"Are we? I still believed that we were coworkers.

"Lily, you are a friend to me, and I want you to think the same of me."

Right, right. You don't do well with emotional things. Don't be shy, officer.

Before asking, Emma rolled her eyes, "What made you not like it all of a sudden?"

Lily stood up from the chair and walked over to the basin to wash her cup. "I knew you would ask this," she said.

"Well? Have you got a response for me?

Both yes and no. Because I am unsure whether that is the correct response or not.

"So just tell me what you have. I may be able to be of assistance. You know, I'm a full-blown lesbian. By default, I am an expert because of it.

Lily laughed, but Emma couldn't see her face since she was facing away from her.

Lily used a handkerchief to wipe the cup dry before turning to face Emma.

"Whatever you said in that lesbian bar was accurate. Actually, the event I had in college wasn't all that horrible. It was a lot of fun. And I was altered by it. It altered me to the point where I became fearful. I believed I was some kind of weirdo. I made a promise to myself that I would never go through that emotion again.

However, why? Did you consider your attraction to women to be odd in any way? enquired Emma.

It wasn't the fact that I was attracted to females that terrified me, but rather the circumstances in which I was most drawn to them and the strength of it, Lily said as she leaned back against the kitchen counter and inhaled deeply.

"I still don't get it," you say.

"All right, I'll just be honest about this or we'll talk about it all night. Three females used deception to get me into their sorority home, where they tested and harassed me. I was horrified at first, but as they went on, I began to feel differently. I experienced a level of pleasure I had never had before, and fairly soon I was encouraging them and yelling for them to be harsher and more cruel. The three girls were fatigued by the time it was all over, but not me.

Emma listened carefully while nodding and straining her eyes.

From that moment on, Tracy—the sexiest, most popular, and lady I was crushing on—became my sex slave. She made advantage of me whenever and whenever she pleased. Even better, she gave me to her lover and instructed me to make him happy. I'm sorry to confess that I did that. All of this began to affect my schoolwork and interfere with my aspirations for me as an addiction. So I just stopped doing everything one day. Since then, I've been trying to avoid having the same emotion come again. I have a partner now, therefore I don't want to get hooked once again.

"Does your boyfriend dominate you in bed?" Asked Emma.

"No, I don't get turned on when a boy dominates me. It is only with girls that I really feel the need to be submissive.

And on that particular day, in the alley, I was more in need than ever.

To be controlled by me?

"Yes."

"So why did you flee? "

"Because I was at my absolute breaking point. I would have also been your slave had I stayed that day. Emma felt a little flutter in her pussy as Lily murmured and her eyes dropped to the floor.

"Since I'm a control freak, Lily, we make a bad mix. I worry about losing all of my senses while being a dominatrix if you worry about being hooked to being a submissive. We were never supposed to be in such close proximity.

Lily responded, "I think the complete opposite," and sheared the satin nightgown strap from her left shoulder.

"Lily, don't do this. You are in a really weak position, and I don't want to take advantage of that.

"I want you to. just time.

Along with the second strap coming down, Emma could no longer resist the young policewoman who was now in front of her.

"I won't...be harsh. See, you get my attention. You truly turn me on, I mean. Emma stood up from the dining table and walked slowly up to Lily, who was leaning against the kitchen counter, her dress just managing to stay on. "Especially right now, oh my god, I just want to eat you up!" exclaimed Emma.

"A kiss is all I have to give you at this time. a tender kiss. a kiss when there is absolutely no dominance. Will that be acceptable to you? Lily and Emma were now interacting directly.

I could care less. All I want is that you treat me whatever you like. even if just a kiss. Emma's robe was untied by Lily, who then showed off her stunning boobs while giving her a slow, sensuous kiss.

Emma inched closer to Lily until their bodies were nearly in contact before giving her a quick kiss on the lips.

I ought to have started off like this sooner. Maybe then you wouldn't have taken off running."

"Screw that. Right now, you are free to do as you choose; I'll stay put.

You don't mind if I put your tongue in my mouth?

in particular if you put my tongue in your mouth.

Emma shoved Lily up against the kitchen counter, totally mashed her body into Lily's, and started sloppily making out with her.

The two policewomen were the epitome of passion and desire, with Emma's hands softly stroking Lily's adorable butt over her dress and her lips nibbling on the tip of Lily's tongue.

Lily was hoisted off her feet and seated on the kitchen counter by Emma as she tightly clutched Lily's waist.

"Lily, you are very lovely. I think you're the only woman I can truly make out with. Fuck, look at these boobs," murmured Emma, carefully removing the nightgown's material to reveal Lily's firm, youthful breasts. "I could just smother them in kisses all night long."

Why don't you do it then? You want to, I know it. I have often seen this expression in your eyes. Officer, I can sense the passion growing inside you.

It's as simple as taking these hands and giving them a little squeeze, Lily said, taking Emma's hands in her own and leading them to her own breasts. similar to this.

When Lily felt Emma's hand on her breasts, she sighed a little before grinning.

Emma was no longer able to contain herself. Lily was the ideal object of want for Emma because of her beauty, kinkiness, and tough appearance. Emma had never previously been so attracted to a young police officer who had just become her partner.

Lily wrapped both of her legs around Emma's waist as she sat on the kitchen counter looking like a doll, while Emma took Lily's nipples in her mouth and started to softly suck on them.

"Officer, your lips feels wonderful on my tits. I've been missing this sensation, fuck. Yessss, the sensation of a woman's soft lips and skin. Now, I'm never going back. I will never refrain from bowing down to a goddess like you.

Emma had ceased paying attention to Lily's words. The younger of the two policewomen sat back on her elbows, closed her eyes, and began massaging Lily's boobs, her lips kissing down her navel, and her tongue licking around Lily's belly button as Emma worked her way down her exquisitely shaped body.

Baby, unwrap your legs from my waist and lay them down on the counter for me. Don't take off your dress, please. Just raise it. You look too lovely in the outfit for me to take it off.

Emma watched the young lady in front of her and let Lily carry out her request. She was so sex-driven that she couldn't think she could control her dominatrix impulses.

The blonde Shakira lookalike didn't want to be violent with the young girl in front of her; instead, she wanted to make love to every part of Lily's body, a sensation she had never had for anyone else.

Lily was distinctive in some way. Ever when Emma first saw the girl at the shooting range, she had known.

"Officer, what are you going to do next? Question the feline between my legs?

"You know very well what I am going to do. You are a police officer as well, aren't you?"

"No, not as good as you! For how many years have you been locking up bad guys behind bars? Huh? You know what they call you in the precinct? The Lioness! And the Lioness is about to wade between my legs. Fuck! How lucky am I?"

How many young policewomen have you fucked, lioness? Lily continued her wordplay as Emma grabbed her toe in her lips and started sucking on it. And how many of them got you as drenched as I did? Has the lioness...aaahhhhh," Lily was forced to scream as Emma licked up her separated legs and kissed her right next to her hot pussy.

Emma's eyes were fixed on Lily as Lily glanced down at her gorgeous face. At that very moment, Lily understood that not even her lover had ever made her feel this way. A wave of pleasure crashed into her crotch.

"Smack me!" Please don't keep waiting. For you, my pussy is aching.

Emma was becoming frustrated with herself. The blonde had no choice but to plunge in since Lily's pussy fragrance had already enchanted her senses.

The instant Emma's lips closed over Lily's pussy, she yelled with delight, and she didn't stop. Nobody paid attention to Lily's hands as they sobbed and threw glasses to the ground.

Emma's tongue continued to snake its way into Lily's pussy as the rain continued to pelt against the window to the two women's left. Lily also continued to scream and groan.

In an effort to gain better access to Lily's pussy, Emma now held both of Lily's legs in her hands and pushed them farther apart. Lily kept her hand on Emma's head and pressed her face more firmly against Emma's cunt as she started to grind her pussy against Emma's face.

'Yes, yes,' Yeeessss..." Bite the skin!" Lily groused. On the sore lips, bite down firmly. Thank you, Emma.

Emma disregarded Lily.

"Pleaseee! I kindly ask. Simply crush your teeth on that sexy cunt of mine. Make me look like a whore. Tell me how you can get me to always extend my legs for you, even if I already have a partner. EMMAAA! PLEASEEE!"

Lily's speech suddenly acquired a tone of madness, and Emma had to stop sucking her pussy. She was slowly reverting to her former habits, and Emma could see it in her eyes that her wants were now progressively taking a hazardous turn.

"Emma, you already know you want to do it. Don't tell yourself lies. I'm yours to have exclusively. Think about it, Emma. Making me your slave, torturing me, and using me. You would adore it, I'm sure. Anytime you want, you may force me to lick your pussy. even when driving our police vehicle. even when the light is red. Simply push me down between your knees while holding my head. You may take me to a budget hotel after each questioning, where you can sit on my face until I suffocate. Emma, don't you want to suffocate me with your wonderful ass? You may not agree with me, but I would like being suffocated by your ass. Yes, I have harbored fantasies about that. And I would love to worship it, if you...just...let...me," said Lily as she parted her legs as far as she could, inserted three of her own fingers in her pussy, and licked each one one by one while gazing lustfully at Emma.

Already losing it, Emma. There was a resurgence of the dominatrix inclinations. At this very moment, all she wanted to do was lift Lily up in her arms, lead her into the bedroom, and rub her sperm all over Lily's beautiful face.

Why are you holding out? Emma, come claim me. Make me yours," Lily said, winking and caressing her pussy simultaneously.

After removing the cum off Lily's fingers one at a time with her lips, Emma stepped closer and gave her a delicate kiss before murmuring in her ear, "No.

Still not. Only when I am confident that you are ready to embrace your crazy, nasty, whorish side will you become my slave. I want to watch you strive for it, plead for it. You are my companion right now and nothing else. Now, you filthy slut, tell me where the dryer is so I can leave you to your perversions.

Lily's eyes widened as she said something Emma couldn't make out beneath her breath.

Lily eventually said, "Get the fuck out of here," and then she closed her eyes.

While Lily remained on the kitchen counter sobbing, Emma grinned, turned around, and left Lily's apartment wearing just a robe.

***

Three days have passed since Emma last saw Lily. When Emma attempted to contact the woman, the phone was off since she had reported ill to the station. Emma had been visiting different dancers for three days, questioning them about how Richard Morrison's guys had either physically abused them or blackmailed them. Emma contemplated seeing Lily for three days before deciding that enough was enough and that Lily had been playing her game for too long on the evening of the third day.

Emma got into her vehicle and drove to Lily's apartment after changing into her regular clothes at the station.

When she arrived, she repeatedly rang the doorbell but no one answered. The door was locked when she attempted to open it.

Emma was now standing at Lily's door, confused and a bit concerned about what she should do next. She struggled to imagine where Lily may have gone when all of a sudden, her boyfriend's home came into focus, and she realized she had to be there.

But she didn't know who he was or where he lived, and now that she realized she didn't know when Lily would be back at work, her want to meet and speak with her rose.

As soon as she had the thought, she ran back to her vehicle, hopped in, and drove off. Her face lit up as she accelerated out of the parking lot, the tires screaming loudly.

***

"Hello? With a plate of waffles in front of her and her usual seat at her favorite café, Emma questioned, "Is this Patrick?"

"Yes, this is Patrick; with whom do I speak?"

Emma Cole, who works with Patrick's girlfriend Lily, introduces herself.

How may I assist you, please? Patrick enquired in a solemn tone.

Lily hasn't arrived at work in four days, Patrick. She had phoned in ill, but we haven't been able to get in touch with her since. She had said that she would only need one day of rest and would return to work as soon as possible, but four days is a long time, so we were understandably concerned. Her phone is also off, so I had to resort to looking through her file to get the emergency contact information she had given us when she joined. Therefore, I was wondering whether you were aware of her location.

After a little period of quiet, Patrick said to Emma, "Lily broke up with me a few days ago, and I haven't heard from her since."

I'm extremely sorry to hear that, Emma responded after gathering her composure after a brief period of shock. But if not a name, at least a phone number of a family member or friend who might know? She admitted to having a nephew. Perhaps the brother-in-law has any information?

Yes, I'll text you his phone number.

That would be really beneficial, Emma added.

"May I ask you a question? Please be understanding of the circumstance I am in, even if I feel a bit strange asking.

"Yes, go ahead, Patrick."

"Well, was there a different male Lily would run into on her patrols, or someone you would see her with, or someone she would mention at work? Since everything between us was wonderful until she joined your precinct, everything changed and she started acting differently. I was hoping you may be familiar with it.

Emma wiped the sweat beads that had started to gather on her forehead with the palm of her hand.

"Patrick, I'm very sorry, but I'm powerless to assist you there. I'm not sure whether it helps or not, but Lily and I spoke mostly about work and she never left my side when we were out on patrols.

"it helps, it helps a lot. Anyway, I appreciate your patience. I'll immediately text you her brother-in-law's phone number.

Patrick, I appreciate that, Emma remarked as she ended the conversation.

Emma drained the glass of water in front of her in one motion and then waited for Patrick to send her a message.

Her phone soon rang, and the unknown number that displayed on the screen.

"Hello?" Fearfully, Emma said.

"Good day, officer. Someone seems to be in a difficult situation.

"Lily? Where the hell are you, dude?

Lily chuckled, "I'm trying to decide whether I truly want to be your slave or not, and it looks like I don't need to be. Perhaps I've already found someone else.

"What the heck are you talking about?"

Say, "Beg for it."

"What?"

"Beg for it if you truly want to know what I'm talking about. I assume that's what you intended me to do. When you abandoned me, leaving me on the kitchen counter with my pussy soaking for you, you left me completely unprepared.

"Listen, stop acting like a child. You haven't been to work in 4 days. You are a new recruit. Are you even serious about your career?" Emma asked, irritated and annoyed.

"I was, until I met you. Now, all I am serious about is becoming your little pet. You won't accept me however. I won't have this career, then. You are to blame, officer.

Cars rushed down Troy Avenue as Emma moaned and watched out the restaurant window.

"Where are you at this moment?"

Say, "Beg for it."

The question "Lily, where are you?"

Say, "Beg for it."

"You realize I can easily get your phone number, right? Brad already received a message about it, and he will send me your whereabouts shortly.

You won't beg, I knew that. You're just much too alpha for that, don't you? I fucking adore you so much because of this. I simply want you to own me, that's all! Nothing needs to be tracked. I have returned to my home. But if you want me to show up to work soon, you'll need to drop by my home for a quick chat. Can you manage it?

"Yes, I'll be there in ten minutes," you said.

"Great. Please make sure to bring back my robe. And when you arrive, please dress warmly. I want to lust after you so much. Lily responded while giggling once more.

Emma thought, "The girl is going insane."

Just as the waitress handed the waffles' bill, she responded, "I am on my way," and hung up.

Two Chapters

When the bike roared to life and Lucy shifted into gear, the wind was already howling around us. However, once it gained momentum and began hurtling through the streets of New York City, the wind launched a vicious attack on my face, pushing my cheeks back and slapping me with gusts that nearly knocked me off the bike.

I gripped Lucy more tightly than I ever had while listening to her giggle from within her helmet.

Lucy was just wearing a short skirt and a bralette, so I imagined how chilly she must be.

I held both of our overcoats in my hands and covered Lucy's breast with one of them while encircling myself with the other.

Lucy said, "I don't want it," and pulled the garment away.

I yelled back in her ears, "You must be really chilly.

I could care less. On my skin, I want to feel the wind.

I had anticipated that. Something made me realize that Lucy was more interested in the excitement of life than she was in heat or cold, and I made a choice at that very moment.

I let go of the coats and clutched them both in a bundle between our bodies, letting the wind wreck havoc on my body.

I complied with Lucy's instructions to "press your chest against my back, hug me tighter, and just allow the wind to whisk you away from stupid thoughts and gloomy places."

She was just wearing a bralette, so when I held her hard, my hands were only a few millimeters below her breasts. I could feel her skin on mine.

The aroma of her hair and the warmth of her body, which infiltrated her flesh and warmed me as well, were the first things I noticed, not the closeness of my hands to her breasts.

I inhaled deeply of her hair before leaning my head on her neck and closing my eyes.

Nothing seemed more liberated than seeing myself weaving through clouds and spiraling into the air above the city, above the suffering, and beyond everything else if I hadn't known any differently.

I got the idea that I was riding a horse with wings and that I was being taken to a location where there were no memories of the previous few years and where the reality of my life had vanished and been replaced with brand-new beginnings.

I sighed and then unintentionally began to caress Lucy's waist on the side.

When Lucy let go of one of the bike's grips and grabbed my hand, she put it directly on top of her left breast and squeezed it. Neither I nor Lucy had any idea that I was doing it.

I was abruptly pulled back to the present as the city sped by, the billboards' flashing lights came into view, and I became aware of what my hands had been doing.

After exhaling, I withdrew my hand.

We both said, "I'm sorry," at the same moment as Lucy slowed the bike enough that we could speak clearly.

"I shouldn't have done that," Lucy said.

"No, I didn't know what I was doing; it simply felt good, but not sexually. Do not see this as a suggestion or anything else.

"I won't," Lucy said, rotating her wrist as she accelerated the bike once again. "Though now that I have experienced what it would be like with you, I don't think I would be able to rest easy," she added.

The remainder of the trip was silent.

We both wanted to enjoy the voyage, so we chose not to speak since neither of us knew what to say.

Unexpectedly, I found myself loving the experience of riding a bike at 100 mph while sitting behind Lucy.

I was no longer bothered by the wind, and this time I did not allow the sensation of soaring over the clouds pass me by.

Because I was so engrossed in the experience, I was unaware when the bike came to a halt. It was only when Lucy caressed my cheeks while holding them on her shoulder that I realized we had arrived.

A spacious, rectangular wooden cottage with a black BMW X5 parked just in front of the entrance was in the center of a clearing surrounded by oak trees as I turned to look around.

I inquired, getting off the bike and straightening my skirt, "Where are we?"

Lucy took off her helmet, her wavy blonde hair dancing in the moonlight, "We are in Woodbury, New York, right on the outskirts of New York City," she said shaking her head.

I peered at the cabin and saw a light in the single visible window.

Whose cabin is this, exactly?

"One of my buddies owns the cottage. She is a budding model who requested me to take some photos of her for her portfolio.

Why did she ask you, exactly?Considering that I am a skilled professional photographer, Amaya. Let me now introduce you to her so that we may have some wine while sitting by the fire. What sound does it make?

That sounds great, but I don't feel good interrupting her picture session in this manner. I remarked, my eyes flitting between the cabin and Lucy, who was fiddling with her skirt and staring at her image in the bike's rearview mirror. "I don't even know her," I muttered.

"She'd be delighted to have you. She is a lovely young lady who is aristocratic like you. I believe you two would get along well.

I sighed and gave a quick nod.

The moon was big and round when I gazed up at the sky. Its light was showering the cabin and the surrounding woodland in silvery tones, shining on the vehicle and the bike's metalwork, and reflecting off Lucy's fair, golden hair.

I shouted and clutched Lucy's hand in terror when a woodchuck scambled across the path as we moved closer to the cabin.

What the heck is happening? A extremely Barbie-esque girl ran frantically from the cabin while seeming afraid.

Lucy gave the child a hug and said, "Nothing, babe, a woodchuck scared our little princess here," which I thought was odd. She then kissed the kid on the lips.

When the girl looked at me and I at her, I was astounded by how beautiful she was.

She resembled a Barbie more than Barbie herself, as I said previously.

One would be wary of touching her for fear of ruining her beauty or destroying the fragility of her very golden hair, which fell straight down her back, past her shoulders, and reached the small of her back and appeared to be made of silk. Her extremely blue eyes were larger than even mine, and they were hidden beneath a canopy of long, curved eyelashes that seemed to go on forever.

I noticed that the girl reminded me of singer and popular Instagram model Loren Gray after carefully examining her characteristics.

"Hi...Amaya? Right?" It's nice to meet you, the girl said as she extended her hand.

"I'm the only one who can enjoy. I'm Mia, and my father owns this little cottage and this photographer's heart. Mia introduced herself and gave Lucy a bear embrace.

"You wish," replied Lucy, giving the blonde a less passionate embrace than she had.

Come, let's get inside before another woodchuck causes Amaya to pass away prematurely.

***

Only the essential necessities were present in the cabin's modestly furnished interior. I was welcomed inside the cabin by a leather sofa, a white rug that spanned half of the space, a table with four seats, a television, some paintings, a kitchenette with some utensils, and a very oddly shaped deer head hanging on the wall.

Lucy sat down on the sofa and said, "There is also a bedroom through that door there, but I don't think any of us would need that."

"Babe, never say never. Our new friend might find the two of us so overwhelming or annoying that she might just need some space to herself, or we might use the bedroom for other extracurricular activities," said Mia, sitting down on one of the wooden chairs and crossing her legs. Her flowy summer dress rode up her thighs and revealed well-toned legs and feet with brightly painted red toenails.

Sorry, but are you two dating each other? I inquired because I couldn't keep the question to myself any longer.

Yes, Lucy, are we a couple?

Lucy stroked her head, "Fuck, you poked the wrong beehive here, Amaya," she muttered.

"Oh, don't worry; I have the solution to this question. We are not dating, Amaya; I am too young to be dating at this time. I just want to sleep with as many people as I can until I get bored and am ready to settle down."

Mia's sarcasm was evident in her voice.

I said, cracking a little smile, "Why do I have a feeling that is not the correct reason."

"Half of it is true; the other half is utter nonsense. She is indeed too young to date. Although I am 25 and she is just 18, the second portion of her response relates more to me than to her. I want to sleep all day long till I become bored.

I pointed at Mia and questioned, "And she wants a relationship?" She was busy looking at her nails and avoiding our eyes, obviously unhappy with the way this talk was going.

Saying, "Let's just say she wants to be exclusive, and I am not ready for it," Lucy turned to face Mia, who had just gotten up from the chair and was approaching a huge hiking pack that was stored in a cabin corner.

She inquired irritably, "Should we start with the photo shoot?"

"Amaya, I believe you could have upset her. She lends you her cabin, after all, and the first thing you do when you arrive is to make her feel awkward. Amaya, that is very unacceptable. Lucy responded, attempting to hold back a giggle, "Shame on you.

"What? No, I didn't intend to...

"Don't worry, Amaya. She's merely playing a joke on you. She enjoys playing pranks on others. I disagree, but she believes it makes her seem hip. She basically comes out looking pitiful, in my opinion.

You realize you're going to pay for that, right? Lucy's eyes widened, and she spoke while gazing at Mia in disbelief. You will now have to put up with Amaya listening to you beg and plead to stop fucking you so hard all night.

When Lucy mentioned fucking the cute, adorable Mia, I had no idea how that would go down. However, when I imagined it, I felt a slight uptick in my heartbeat and realized I wanted to witness that happen in front of my eyes. You would think that after spending about four hours with Lucy, I would be used to her audacious statements and remarks, but I wasn't.

I was eager to watch the charming, endearing Mia, age 18, stretched wide by a strap.

What the heck was going on with me?

Beginning the picture session, Mia sat on the floor with her back against the wall, her arms up in the air, ample cleavage on display, and the most seductive looks imaginable while wearing her purple sundress.

When Mia changed stances, Lucy to her right, who was laying flat on her stomach, caught every movement with her DSLR camera.

One thing was very evident to me when I watched my first live picture session from a sofa.

I saw a shift in myself.

My physique had undergone a change.

Since Steve and I had broken up six months prior, I had made a concerted effort to arouse my sexual desire by watching a lot of porn, buying sex toys that resembled futuristic laser guns more than actual sex toys, and even engaging in a little phone sex, but my body had never responded as I had hoped.

When I thought I was on the verge of having an orgasm, something in my thoughts would kick in and my body would refuse to comply.

But ever since I met Lucy, my body has chosen to get excited at the most unexpected of times. My pussy would tingle and beg to be touched at the most inconvenient of times, and even now, as I stared at the curve of Lucy's ass as she lay flat on her stomach with her skirt doing a terrible job of covering her ass cheeks, and as I watched the young Mia arching her body against the wall of the cabin while making love to the camera with eyes the color

I looked away from the picture session and down at my feet as the mere notion made me start to perspire.

Then, when I heard Lucy urge Mia to cover her breasts with her hands and heard the rustling of clothing, my resolve was shattered and I was forced to glance at Mia once again. What I saw made my pussy ache so fiercely that I felt real anguish at being unable to caress it.

Mia had loosened the dress' straps, baring her breasts, which she had since covered with her hands. She was coyly glancing into the camera while flashing a sinister grin that could make corpses come to life.

Mia was encouraged by Lucy to say, "Beautiful...Perfect babe...you look absolutely amazing," which caught my attention. Lucy was making no attempt to hide her hips, which were now clearly exposed.

"Can I go outside to take a stroll around the cabin?" My voice cracked as I questioned. Even in the midst of October, my throat felt as parched as the Sahara, and I was perspiring.

When Lucy and Mia both turned to face me, Lucy did not reveal what she was thinking, but she raised an eyebrow and said, "Why do you want to go? Are you enjoying yourself? Were you bored with us?

I said, gesturing to Mia, "No, not at all. In fact, I am quite excited by all of this. However, I just need some fresh air and I want to explore the neighborhood a little bit, if it is safe.

Yes, it is rather safe, but given that a woodchuck scared you, Lucy added, "I just don't know what else might frighten you."

I tried to sound certain when I answered, "Don't worry, I will be fine," but the trembling in my voice revealed my uneasiness.

Lucy smiled comfortingly, "Okay, just give a shout if you feel alone...or scared," and I nodded.

The moon was hiding behind a few stray clouds outside, and the trees were softly swaying in the breeze, creating a darker woodland than the one that had first welcomed me.

I just went up to where the bike was parked since I dared not go too far from the cabin.

I stroked the bike's leather seat with my hands before circling it and petting the gas tank while I took in the surrounding woodland.

Even though I knew I was in a dream and that this was not real, I continued to sleep and tried to make it go as long as I could out of dread of waking up and interrupting the idly occurring experience.

I wondered who Mia was as I turned to face the cabin; in fact, I also wondered who Lucy was because I didn't know much about her other than the fact that she was a feisty young lesbian with detailed tattoos on the side of her neck, who could kick ass and ride fast motorbikes.

Then, as I made my way to the edge of the clearing and turned to face the still-dark trees in front of me, a thought that had been bothering me ever since I had seen Lucy curled up on the ground clicking Mia in her alluring mood came to me.

Was I progressively discovering that I wasn't straight?

Had I discovered an aspect of myself that had been dormant for all these years after meeting a very assertive, strong girl who was interested in other women?

I pictured kissing Lucy as I strolled around the edge of the clearing, sometimes touching the tree bark and feeling the rough, jagged texture of the wood.

I stopped moving and, while closing my eyes, visualized putting my body against Lucy's and placing my hands on her waist.

My heart went into overdrive just from the sight of her, and I hadn't even considered giving her a kiss.

In my imagination, she continued to run her hands through my hair before suddenly pulling my face in toward hers and placing her lips against them. Something told me that this must have been how Lucy made love to other women, so I continued to picture her doing the same thing to me.

A voice called out, "Amaya?"

When I opened my eyes, Mia was standing at the cabin door, looking at me and said, "We're done. Do you want some wine?

"Yes," I answered.

"All right, go inside now. I'll give you some to eat. Mia made a U-turn and went inside the cabin.

As I entered, I saw Mia and Lucy seated on the rug, facing each other, holding glasses of red wine, and conversing softly.

But as soon as I walked in, the two females instantly stopped chatting and gave me strange looks.

Mia patted the chair next to her and invited Amaya to join her.

"Okaayyy..." A glass of red wine was ready for me when I joined the ladies on the rug after saying something and looked from Lucy to Mia.

Without saying a word, Mia grabbed the glass from her and gave it to me.

What were you two discussing? I questioned as I sipped, noticing the liquid's harshness on the tip of my tongue.

Mia said, "We were talking about you," while Lucy quietly sipped her beverage and stared at me inquisitively.

And why were you mentioning me?

"About how charming you are, fascinating you are, and good natured you are..." Finally speaking, Lucy leaned back on her hands.

"How do you know I'm a good person? I tried to equal Lucy's intensity as I returned her look, but I scarcely knew anything about her.

Oh, I see. You are the kind of lady that makes you fall in love. This sort of women, Mia, is the one you should pursue. I'm a hopeless case, but not this lady. You can bet your bottom dollar that if she likes you, she will stay in love with you until the day you pass away.

I flushed and hid my face behind my hands, saying, "Okay, stop elevating me to such a position. In fact, you are the only one who has been nice tonight. by first salvaging my night and then saving me from that club jerk.

Lucy said, "But it hasn't been saved yet."

Oh, it was spared. I said, taking another large swallow of the wine and making a grimace as it passed down my neck. "I already feel like I'm having more fun than I was at the club," I said.

"However, I kept my word to give you more, and trust me, this is just the beginning. Why don't we have a game?" Suddenly aroused, Lucy glanced at Mia, then at me, raising her eyebrows as she said.

I questioned, "What game?"

"A basic one. Each of us shares the one thing that, if it were to come true, would make them the happy right now. These wishes must not be unrealistic; for example, Mia cannot wish for larger breasts. Lucy giggled as she said this, and Mia blinked in surprise. Many of the physicians I know in Los Angeles would disagree with you.

Mia was given a kiss on the lips by Lucy, who then said, "I was just kidding, doll.

When my pussy began to pulse once again, I wished Lucy had kissed me instead of someone else.

I already knew what I would say, "I'm in."

Mia responded, "I'll go first. I'd love to know her story," and she made a head-pointing gesture at me.

The question "My story?"

I just want to know what it is. "Yes, I mean, from what Lucy has told me, you came into the club tonight to start new, to forget a specific element of your life that has been bothering you.

Drinking her wine slowly, Lucy grinned, "Looks like we might just become a lot closer than you expected, Amaya."

What if I refuse?

The sneer would not leave Lucy's face as she warned, "Well, then I will take back all the praise that I had showered on you earlier, and you will be expelled from this cabin and given over to the kingdom of woodchucks who will then torture you to death."

Okay, but be aware that it will soon be my time, and you could find yourself in the same circumstance.

I'm willing to take that opportunity, Lucy stated with assurance.

"About six months ago, I saw my closest buddy giving my fiancé a blowout in front of me. My fiancé—with whom I have a child—got a blowjob from my best friend, who was meant to be my maid of honor, and the two of them are now on their honeymoon in the Maldives. My fiance was due to marry me in three weeks.

Oh my, that's horrible. I could see Lucy was working very hard not to laugh when she remarked, "That is extremely horrible.

I heard myself saying, "It isn't that funny once it happens to you," as my fury grew.

"I'm not sure. You've got to agree it's a bit amusing, Lucy replied, before she eventually started laughing and slammed her fist on the floor with her wine flowing over the side.

What I was witnessing beyond belief. I had anticipated some sorrow or compassion, but this girl was laughing heartily at my misfortune with no regard for her reputation or any repercussions.

I muttered, attempting to contain my rage as I looked at Lucy with bloodshot eyes and said, "I suppose I may have judged you too hastily.

Lucy abruptly ceased to laugh.

I briefly believed that I had awoken the beast within of her as her eyes met mine and she scampered up to me on all fours. I feared that I would get the same treatment as the guy at the club.

Lucy didn't strike me however.

Your time, she said as she came to a halt a few inches from me, her eyes still fixed on mine. What would bring you the most joy at this moment?

"I'm aware of your saga, Lucy. I'm curious as to how you came to be who you are.

Lucy was still on all fours, pushing forward, her lips a few millimeters from mine. She said, "You don't want to go down that path."

Lucy was as calm as a cucumber, while I was laboring to breathe.

Mia sat enjoying her wine while carefully observing our back and forth.

"I think I want to," I affirmed.

"When my parents committed suicide, I was two years old. While I was in my cradle, my father murdered my mother and then shot himself in the head a short distance away. They discovered me playing with my mother's corpse, clawing at her face while grinning naively, completely naïve to the horror I was about to be thrown into. After being brought to an orphanage, I was quickly adopted by a guy. A insane guy who adopted me with the sole intent of turning me into a beautiful lady, after which he would rape me daily until I could scarcely feel his dick inside of me. And then one day, while he was dying in front of me, I shot him with his pistol. He then snatched the rifle from my hand and shot myself as well. I was on the verge of passing out when Lucy grabbed my hand and put it on the back of her leg. "This is the wound from that bullet," she murmured, her eyes piercing into mine.

Mia spoke the words, "Enough, I think that is enough for tonight."

"What? I was unable to express what would bring me the most joy. Lucy backed away from me and sat down in her former seat, emptying the wine glass all at once, saying, "This is not fair, ladies.

My thoughts had started to become consumed with worry, and my heart was racing rapidly in my chest.

I didn't like how Lucy was acting, and I could see from Mia's eyes that she was a bit concerned as well.

Okay, Lucy, tell me what would make you the happiest.

I was simply pleased that she had moved her focus away from me as Lucy turned her head to gaze at Mia.

Lucy yelled, "I would love...to....go down on you right now, baby," and swung at Mia.

Lucy grabbed the little girl and pushed her to her back on the mat, where she straddled Mia's little waist between her thighs and began frantically kissing her.

I watched in wonder and awe as Mia began kissing Lucy back, attempting to equal Lucy's fervor. Mia's response was faster than I had anticipated.

The two females rolling about on the ground while muttering into each other's mouths was the most sensuous scene I had ever seen.

Mia was content to play the part of the submissive as Lucy's tongue devoured her lips, showing that Lucy was definitely the dominant one or the "top" since she made sure she was always in charge of the kiss.

As Lucy grabbed hold of Mia's breast and flattened her full palm on the fabric of her summer dress, she began sucking on Mia's tongue. I witnessed Lucy do this.

Mia held Lucy while letting her entirely control her lips and body. Lucy's groans were desperation-filled, and Mia's eyes were closed.

The summer dress was torn to bits when Lucy took hold of the front and tore it down the center.

I saw Mia gritting her teeth ferociously as she yelled.

"Amaya, you are now free to enter the bedroom. While keeping her gaze fixed on Lucy, Mia warned that things may just get a bit too crazy for her.

"No, she'll remain here. I'll fuck you raw in front of her, Mia. She'll just sit there and watch while you're destroyed. I am sure that is exactly what she wants, isn't it?" Lucy looked at me, and my knees went weak.

Currently, Lucy was experiencing her most primitive phase.

I imagined what it would be like to have her on top of me in this state—her hair was untidy, her eyes were blazing with unquenchable need, and she was breathing heavily—and my pussy responded by unexpectedly getting extremely wet.

I remained silent instead of responding to Lucy and continued gazing at her. Lucy grinned before turning to face Mia and smirking, "See, she wants to watch."

Then, while Lucy giggled, Mia said, "Then we have to make sure we give her a good show," and, as if suddenly overcome with a storm of sexual desires, she began wildly kissing Lucy's neck, licking and biting her skin like a maniac, before saying, "Don't you worry about giving her a good show, you leave that to me. All you have to do is lay down and stretch your legs out for me, Mucy said, before grabbing the underneath of Mia's thighs and giving her a firm nudge to separate her legs so they could be kissed along the side.

The sight of the gorgeous, barbie-like girl, with her legs spread wide on the floor and her summer dress dangling from her body, being torn to pieces by an equally beautiful blonde, who was licking her silky smooth skin, her saliva glistening on the surface, leaving a trail from her thigh to her feet, was too much for me. Mia arched her back, just like she had done while she was getting clicked, but this time, she was also biting her juicy

All I wanted to do was reach down and stroke my pussy with my hand.

I wanted to fuck myself as I saw the two gorgeous women in front of me fall madly in love and want for one another. I also wanted to beg them to rip my clothing off of me and demonstrate what it was like to have a female suck my pussy.

But despite how fiercely the fire inside of me raged, I controlled myself. I was horny, but not horny enough to let go of all restraints and ultimately go into the uncharted waters of girl on girl sex.

The two females had ceased focusing on me. While Lucy was taking her sweet time, the younger of the two was eagerly waiting for the elder one to plunge between her legs.

Lucy was playing with the Barbie, bathing her flesh in saliva while keeping her gaze, gently nibbling on her toe and then licking her heel.

"You see, Amaya, I would be happy to be her boyfriend, and I would be happy to abandon all the beautiful females in the world for this young woman here, but I know I would exploit her in a very self-centered way. I'll take full advantage of her alluring beauty, and in doing so, I may just go beyond the limits I've set for myself. After all, just look at her: her supple, youthful body; her buttery smooth legs; and the pussy I'm going to devour. Who wouldn't want to give their all to spend just one night with this beauty?"

As Lucy moved towards the middle of Mia's legs, feeling the softness of her skin as she kissed her way up her thighs, and eventually reaching her pussy, Mia groaned and flung her hands back.

Do you want a lick? As if serving me dessert, Lucy abruptly stopped, turned to face me, and said.

I didn't respond right away. When all I wanted was a lick, how could I? I wanted to nod strongly, but once again, I was paralyzed by dread of the repercussions and the implications of really committing to this, so all I could muster was a very weak "no."

With a giggle that was almost cruel and nasty, Lucy once again began licking Mia's thighs' inner surfaces.

Just gobble me up, please. Please just fuck do it, Mia pleaded, kicking the air with her legs in a lovely display of desperation.

Mia's feet were now behind her head, Lucy's legs were in the air, and her pussy was directly in front of her, as well as directly in front of me. Lucy grinned and then grasped both of Mia's ankles.

I had never before seen a vagina that wasn't my mine.

Yes, I had previously seen porn, but I had always made an effort to focus on the guy and his dick rather than the female and her vagina.

Mia had a shaved pussy that was shimmering with her secretions. I licked my lips and slid closer to Mia to have a better look while staring at her vagina like a thirsty hound. Her pussy lips weren't particularly thick, but just enough to provide an opportunity to lick and suck them intensely.

Holding Mia's knees and sometimes kissing the bottom of her feet, Lucy remarked, "You like what you see?"

Yes, I've never seen one just like that.

"Pretty? You probably have a lovely one as well. As Lucy slid between Mia's knees and began licking her pussy passionately, she added matter-of-factly, "I bet your tastes better than any pussy in the world," and Mia instantly lost control.

Mia's hands began to flail, and she began yelling hysterically at the sensation of Lucy's lips pushing on her pussy and the touch of her tongue on her cunt.

However, Lucy paid little attention to the impact she was having on the 18-year-old. In the throes of passion, Lucy herself had become insane, and she began sucking and licking Mia's pussy as vigorously as she could.

With her eyes closed and her face flat on Mia's crotch, Lucy was a beast set loose. Her tongue danced over Mia's pussy and slithered into the folds of her vagina, licking the walls within.

Mia glanced away, and then she turned to face me.

She offered me her hand in a holding motion.

I paused and then froze.

"Amaya, please hold me. If I can't expect to obtain anything else from you, I would simply be content holding your hand and cuddling since you are so gorgeous. Please, oh my goodness, please.

Mia took my outstretched hand securely in hers before throwing her head back in pleasure.

Mia raised her ass off the mat and let out a loud moan only a few seconds after I had held her hand.

Her eyes widened, and without any provocation, she immediately put my palm on her lips and began kissing my fingers.

As Lucy began to finger her cunt and tease her clit with her tongue, Mia took my thumb in her mouth and began to suck on it hard.

"Yessss Lucy...Amayaa...Lucy...yessss." Mia would alternately scream our names, and I didn't know what to do.

My brain had reached a new level after hearing Mia call my name in a lovely voice as her saliva glistened on my finger. At that point, my desires finally burst through the barriers that had been keeping them in check, and what I did next shocked not only me but also Mia.

Mia quickly gave me a passionate kiss while nibbling on my bottom lip with hunger as I went closer and thrust my lips into hers.

Then she arrived.

She had a loud and powerful orgasm.

In response, Lucy began to chuckle as she saw the young model come all over her face as her body twitched and she pushed Lucy's face between her legs and began shoving her crotch into her lips.

Lucy continued to giggle even after Mia's climax faded and I broke the kiss since she was obviously enjoying herself and drinking wine.

When I finally realized what I had done, I stumbled back in shock and terror, which made Lucy laugh even louder than usual.

"I suppose I finally succeeded in preserving your evening, didn't I?" Lucy questioned as she turned to face me before stooping to embrace Mia tightly.

When Stella and Peyton approached the pub, it was almost empty. The only patrons the girls could see were two young college students working on their computers, a guy seated at the bar, and an elderly man lounging in the shadows smoking a cigar.

Stella, who was following Peyton inside the pub, saw the young cop turn to look at the two college students seated at the corner table working on their Macbooks.

Stella had a peek at them as well and noted how lovely each of the girls were.

One of them was a redhead who resembled Amber Heard from Aquaman sans the scales and gills, while the other was a blonde with spectacles, very little freckles, but quite large breasts.

Stella inquired as the two snatched a seat just a few feet away from the females, "You like them, don't you?"

Yes, they are quite adorable.

Do you believe you will make a move on them?

"Hit them on? Oh no, not when the bar's sexiest lady is already seated next to me, but I'd want to know whether you think they're adorable.

Stella took another glance at the women and could not help but agree that they were both wonderfully attractive and seductive in their tank tops and booty shorts, but she also believed that she was already seated next to the sexiest woman in the pub.

Stella said, "They're cute, but you're cuter."

"Stella, don't attempt to dodge the subject. Which one do you prefer? Please tell me.

Question: "Do I have to?"

Yep, I'm insistent. I kept you alive. The very least you can do for me is that.

Stella cracked under the strain and turned to look at the girls again, this time really observing them, hearing them giggle, and then observing their blue and green eyes look at the computer screen with concentration. She realized she preferred the blonde with the freckles to the other girl by a tiny bit.

It's "The blonde."

"Really? Why? Considering that she is the

youngest of the two? Stella asked Peyton with a wink, "Do you like young girls, Peyton? " She could clearly see that the alcohol was beginning to affect the cop.

"Peyton, I don't even believe I like females. It was all in good fun. Stella made a joke, "I guess you want the blonde for yourself.

"No! How can I ignore a redhead? Do you have any idea how wild they become in bed? They have the power to ruin your morals. Woman!" Peyton said before turning her head to once more glance at the females and licking her lips.

Stella was beginning to worry since the girls had seen Peyton sexily observing them, and she did not want to put herself through any more anxiety.

The waitress inquired for their orders as soon as she approached their table.

"Peyton, you said you were not interested in them!" Stella yanked Peyton's hand after placing an order for two drinks for the two of them.

No, I wasn't! But you just stated that you aren't

interested in me, and I told you that I get horny when I'm drunk, so if I can't have you, why can't I try on that gorgeous redhead over there?" Peyton said, pointing directly at the girl, who was now obviously extremely uncomfortable.

Stella said, "Peyton, I don't think the girls are liking what you are doing," as the redhead grinned in their general direction and the blonde murmured in her ear.

"I believe you are mistaken! Stella, did you see that smile? Stella was forced to touch her crotch from under her pants by Peyton, who grabbed Stella's hand and stated, "Fuck, that girl has gotten me so wet, check it out! "

When the girls saw what Peyton was doing, Stella flushed and her eyelids drooped.

Both females stood up and began to go toward Stella and Peyton's table when the blonde laughed.

Hey there gentlemen, mind if we join you?" the blonde inquired.

"No, honey, of course not. If you hadn't come to us, I would have contacted you, Peyton added.

Stella only grinned.

The blonde Trisha introduced herself as "Kelly" and stated, "My name is Trisha."

"My name is Peyton, and this is Stella, who appears to be 28 but is actually 36," Peyton said.

Stella frowned at Peyton, but the blonde responded with a grin and a question in her eyes: "Really? It just so happens that I'm weak to older ladies.

Trisha, the blonde, continued to stare at Stella with a sly smirk on her face as Stella started to feel her hands start to sweat.

Stella was baffled as to why two females had just chosen to approach their table and begin flirting with them.

They were indeed at a lesbian bar, right?

"Well, lady, this is your fortunate day. As soon as Stella entered the pub, she had feelings for you. Stella watched Peyton's hand go around Kelly's waist and Stella heard her say, "I would love to fuck the straightness out of that blonde," as Peyton glanced at me and added.

Stella was astounded by Peyton's actions.

Peyton had been acting like the most responsible, self-assured, and level-headed person Stella had ever seen for two nights, but now that she had alcohol in her system, she had suddenly turned into a perverse, lecherous girl who was horny for every lady she saw.

She's not required to do that. I've always been homosexual. Trisha stated, her eyes still roving Stella's body and lingered over her boobs for longer than Stella anticipated. "I thought that was a given since we are sitting in a lesbian bar," Stella said.

We're at a lesbian bar, right? Stella turned to face Peyton, who was now caressing the redhead's boobs as the redhead sat giggling and her eyes were closed in ecstasy. Peyton's hand had into the redhead's top.

I apologize, Stella. It is an ingrained force. Because I am unaware of any other bars, I must have taken us to a lesbian pub.

Trisha moved closer to Stella and questioned, "Why do you seem upset?" while maintaining her hand on her thigh.

Stella felt her heart begin to pound like war drums and her pulse increase.

Her pussy suddenly sprang alive as she felt the lovely blonde's touch on her thigh.

Peyton caught her attention as she was tenderly kissing Kelly's lips after turning her face to face with her.

Trisha queried, her blue eyes waiting impatiently for them to begin making out as well. "Is something wrong?" she questioned Stella.

Stella eventually said, "Yes, I am not into women," to which Peyton abruptly put an end to their kissing and turned to stare at Stella in astonishment.

"I apologize. You are a lovely girl, I know that, but I don't believe I can pull this off.

Trisha questioned, "Why are you in a lesbian bar in the first place?"

"Because I wasn't aware that it was a lesbian bar."

"What should I do at this point? Your buddy and my friend are both busy. Are we merely meant to stare at one another?

Peyton responded, "No, you can join us too," and reached across the table to hold Trisha's hand.

Stella saw Peyton slowly escape her clutches and felt her heart sink as she realized it was time to go.

Leaving the table and standing. Stella grinned as she cast a glance at Peyton, who was still tucking her hand under Kelly's top.

"Peyton, I want to thank you for all you have done for me. You were a godsend to me when you entered my life, and I doubt I'll ever be able to pay you back.

As Peyton's fingers encircled Kelly's areola and then squeezed her nipple under her blouse, the stunning redhead winced before giggling and responding, "You can repay me by staying," Peyton added.

I'm sorry, but I'm unable to accomplish that.

"I perceive. Be the prude you want to be if you want to be one. When Peyton was ready to continue, Trisha reached over the table, kissed her, silencing her, and then looked at Stella as if to say, "Look what you missed out on. I'll see you tomorrow to tell you about my interrogation."

Stella exited the pub into the pouring rain with a heavihearted "Bye," since any thoughts of a relationship with Peyton that went beyond friendship had vanished from her mind.

***

Stella often went to the Western Haven Park, which was just across from her apartment, when she had a lot on her mind.

The next morning at six in the morning, Stella was sitting on a park bench, watching a bunch of young boys play soccer.

Stella's blonde hair was flirting with the cold breeze flowing through the park as the sun had just begun to rise over the horizon, coloring the edges of the sky scarlet. Frank Sinatra was singing in his mesmerizing voice via her headphones.

Stella waited impatiently for Peyton to begin questioning the intruder to her chamber.

Stella was hoping Peyton would make sure that everything was done to find the offender despite the fact that she knew the guy would have been coached to keep his mouth shut and that there were various methods for police to persuade someone to speak.

It took Stella some time to notice she was being tapped on the shoulder as she was lost in her own thoughts and watched the lads throw the ball about.

Turning her head, Peyton was seated next to her on the bench wearing sports leggings and a sports bra, with AirPods in her ears and her arms and forehead dripping with perspiration.

"Peyton?"

Why do you seem so shocked to see me, yes?

Stella said, "I didn't anticipate you to be up this early today.

Why is that, then?

Naturally, I had anticipated some nighttime events to occur yesterday after I had left the pub. Have the females already left? Or are they still in your room sleeping while you are out and about?

"The girls never made it to my room," Peyton said.

"What? You dropped the ball on a threesome?"

"I was present for it. The girls were eager to get started. They were never invited to my home by me.

I ask, "But why?"

I have no clue, to be honest," Peyton said as she took a big breath and turned away from Stella to gaze at the lads who had just celebrated a goal. Something inside of me urged me not to go further with this. I believe that I had some remorse about leaving you. Additionally, I want to apologize for being nasty. I referred to you as a prude, right?

"You did, indeed. And I'm not going to lie—I felt a bit wounded.

And Stella, I'm really sorry about it. I always regret the things I do after drinking, whether for many days or just the following day. I've changed my life in a lot of ways, but there is one thing I can't seem to get over. You must realize that although I am not trying to explain what I did by attributing everything to drink, I am just as frustrated with this situation as you are.

Stella saw Peyton's apparent vulnerability as she stared at her. The lady who had knocked on her door two days before was certain, courageous, and seemed to have it all figured out, but the girl sitting next to her was undeveloped, fragile, and appeared to also be in need of assistance.

I would not have given you whiskey on the first day of our meeting if I had known you were attempting to give up booze.

It's OK. You are not at blame.

As the sun rose higher in the sky, the two ladies watched the soccer match for a while.

You don't like females, then? Peyton finally mustered the guts to ask Stella the query that had been bugging her.

"As I already told you, I have no idea."

You may have found out about it yesterday.

Stella looked into Peyton's light brown eyes, which were shimmering from the sun. "But I had told you, I want to try it out with someone I know, or someone I am comfortable with," she said.

Stella wondered, "Why don't you understand that it is only you that quickens my pulse and makes my pussy throb like never before."

A: "What about me?" Peyton enquired while keeping her voice cool and locking eyes with Stella.

"How are you doing?"

Would you feel at ease with me?

Stella's heart began to beat more quickly as her eyes widened.

Stella lowered her voice and said, "I don't know," flushing more than she had anticipated. She turned her head away from Peyton's face, who was still staring at Stella with a strong and assured expression on her face.

Peyton nearly bullied Stella with her eyes as she continued, "I think you might be comfortable with me."

Stella began to take deep breaths and experienced a little increase in anxiousness.

Stella managed to remark, "I like you."

Do you feel okay? Peyton moved closer to Stella while holding onto her arm.

"I don't know what caused me to suddenly feel so worried. With a shaky voice and trembling hands, Stella remarked, "I'm older than you, yet I behave weaker.

You are not required to respond to this question at this time, and we may end our chat at this point if you want.

"No, I like this discussion. I don't want to forget it, but when someone confides in me like this, I am quite uneasy. I've had terrible losses in the past, and as a result, I have a highly pessimistic outlook on placing my confidence in others.

"I get it, Stella. I won't yell at you. Now that you are aware of my feelings for you, the initiative is in your hands.

You know where to find me if you ever want to pique your interest.

Stella nodded, wondering why it was becoming harder and harder for her to tell Peyton that she, too, was dying to kiss her right this second.

However, something was preventing her.

Was her marriage a failure?

Was it as a result of the recent close call with rape?

"Would you like to come up for some coffee?" Stella enquired, attempting to change the subject of the discussion.

"I would love to," Peyton added.

***

The remainder of the morning was spent by the ladies conversing with one another over coffee and Stella's homemade waffles, which Pcyton could not stop complimenting.

Why did you work as a waitress? You ought to be a chef! Peyton carefully licked her fingers as she added, "I've tasted waffles at the restaurant you used to work, and I'm sure these waffles you've cooked are much better than the trash they used to serve over there.

Why are you gazing at me?

Stella made an attempt at flirting and stated, "I liked the way you were licking your fingers."

"Really? You'll like it even more when I suck my fingers clean of your come.

When Stella heard it, she almost spat her coffee out, and Peyton started laughing.

I apologize; that was a touch too direct.

It's OK. I won't like that, I can't deny it," Stella replied.

"See, now that you say things like that, I have to question whether you're attempting to conceal the truth. It is OK to enjoy the company of persons of the same gender. You could just be somewhat lesbian and not even entirely bisexual.

I have nothing against those who like someone of their own gender, Peyton. I have always had a strong sense of solidarity with the LGBTQ community. But the truth is that I already have a lot on my plate. I am jobless, I have a crazy, powerful guy who wants to rape me, and I can't add anything more to that.

Peyton questioned, biting her bottom lip and leaning her head to one side. "What if this isn't something that will add to your stress, but help you relax?" she said.

The question "What are you doing?" Stella enquired while grinning.

"Why? Peyton questioned as her attitude abruptly changed, "Did I look weird doing that?"

"No, you were adorable."

However, I was aiming for sexy.

"Peyton, you don't need to strive to be seductive. You are the sexiest policewoman I have ever seen, a towering, alpha-feminine, gun-toting supermodel.

Oh my gosh, I've never received such a praise.

If so, you've been socializing with the wrong crowd.

"Well, don't hold it against me. People who should know better are nonetheless unclear about their sexual orientation.

Let's see what we can do about it, Stella grinned and agreed.

Yes, but I have to go back to my house to change into my uniform before going to question the burglar of your home.

Stella said, "Okay," as her worries reappeared.

"Would you like to accompany me?"

"I'm not sure if I want to deal with that man once more."

The need won't arise. There is a beach nearby. I could deliver you there. Right now, there are a lot of people at the beach. You may stroll about and take in the feel of the sand under your feet; before you know it, I'll be back with some happy news. It won't take long, in my opinion.

Stella questioned, "Why are you so sure that it will be good news and that it won't take long?"

"Let's just say I've gotten off to a good start. After that, I'll tell you more. Please change out of the pants and shirt and wear something that accentuates your physique a little more before I return to pick you up in about an hour. It will be useful to me throughout the questioning.

Stella responded in an irate tone, "How the hell will me wearing a revealing dress help your interrogation?" while seeming frustrated.

"It is challenging. Just do it, would you?

In her sexiest voice, Stella replied, "As you say, officer."

Peyton just let out a long sigh before shaking her head.

Peyton was thinking as she left her residence, "The things I will do to you, Stella, when I get my hands on you."

www.ingramcontent.com/pod-product-compliance
Lightning Source LLC
Chambersburg PA
CBHW050414120526
44590CB00015B/1961